D1550220

Susan

From

GIOVANNA PIPIA

Date

Sept 27 /2006

PROMISES & PRAYERS

for
Moms

SECOND EDITION

PROMISES
&PRAYERS

for
Moms

Scripture quotations are taken from:

The Holy Bible, King James Version

The Holy Bible, New International Version (NIV) Copyright © 1973, 1978, 1984, by International Bible Society. Used by permission of Zondervan Publishing House. All rights reserved.

The Holy Bible, New King James Version (NKJV) Copyright © 1982 by Thomas Nelson, Inc. Used by permission.

The New American Standard Bible®, (NASB) Copyright © 1960, 1962, 1963, 1968, 1971, 1972, 1973, 1975, 1977, 1995 by The Lockman Foundation. Used by permission.

Holy Bible, New Living Translation, (NLT) Copyright © 1996. Used by permission of Tyndale House Publishers, Inc., Wheaton, Illinois 60189. All rights reserved.

New Century Version®. (NCV) Copyright © 1987, 1988, 1991 by Word Publishing, a division of Thomas Nelson, Inc. All rights reserved. Used by permission.

The Message (MSG)- This edition issued by contractual arrangement with NavPress, a division of The Navigators, U.S.A. Originally published by NavPress in English as THE MESSAGE: The Bible in Contemporary Language copyright 2002-2003 by Eugene Peterson. All rights reserved.

Revised Standard Version. (RSV) Copyright © 1946, 1952, 1959, 1973 by the Division of Christian Education of the National Council of the Churches of Christ in the United States of America. All rights reserved. Used by permission.

The Holman Christian Standard Bible™ (HCSB) Copyright © 1999, 2000, 2001 by Holman Bible Publishers. Used by permission.

Cover Design by Kim Russell / Wahoo Designs
Page Layout by Bart Dawson

ISBN 1-58334-238-9

Printed in the United States of America

FAMILY
CHRISTIAN
PRESS

Table of Contents

Introduction

ecause you're reading this book, you probably answer to the name "Mom," "Mother," "Mommy," or some variation thereof—if so, congratulations. As a loving mother, you have been blessed by your children and by God.

Perhaps you received this book as a gift from a devoted child or husband. Or perhaps, amid the hustle and bustle of your day, you managed to pick up this little book of your own accord. Either way, you will be blessed if you take the promises on these pages to heart.

This text addresses 71 topics of intense interest to Christian mothers. Each brief chapter contains Bible verses, a quotation from a noted Christian thinker, and a prayer. The ideas in each chapter are powerful reminders of God's commandments and of the joy that He promises His children.

Motherhood is both a priceless gift from God and an unrelenting responsibility. This book is intended to remind you that when it comes to the tough job of being a responsible mother, you and God, working together, are destined to do great things for your kids and for the world.

Abundance

And God is able to make all grace abound to you,
so that always having all sufficiency in everything,
you may have an abundance for every good deed.

2 Corinthians 9:8 NASB

These things have I spoken unto you, that my joy
might remain in you, and that your joy might be full.

John 15:11 KJV

Success, success to you, and success to those who help you,
for your God is with you . . . .

1 Chronicles 12:18 NIV

Enjoy serving the Lord,
and he will give you what you want.

Psalm 37:4 NCV

I am come that they might have life,
and that they might have it more abundantly.

John 10:10 KJV

*G*od sent His Son so that mankind might enjoy the abundant life that Jesus describes in the familiar words of John 10:10. But, God's gifts are not guaranteed; His gifts must be claimed by those who choose to follow Christ. As you organize your day and care for your family, accept God's promise of spiritual abundance. Those who accept that promise and live according to God's commandments are eternally blessed.

God is the giver, and we are the receivers.
And His richest gifts are bestowed not upon
those who do the greatest things, but
upon those who accept His abundance
and His grace.

Hannah Whitall Smith

– A Prayer –

Thank You, Dear Lord, for the abundant life that is mine through Your Son Jesus. In all that I say and do, let me share Your message of abundance with my family, my friends, and my community. Give me courage, Lord, to claim the spiritual riches that You have promised, and help me to share Your abundance with all who cross my path.

Amen

Accepting Christ

*This is how much God loved the world: He gave his Son,
his one and only Son. And this is why: so that no one need
be destroyed; by believing in him anyone can have
a whole and lasting life.*

John 3:16 MSG

*If you confess with your mouth, "Jesus is Lord," and
believe in your heart that God raised Him from the dead,
you will be saved. With the heart one believes,
resulting in righteousness, and with the mouth one confesses,
resulting in salvation.*

Romans 10:9, 10 HCSB

*And there is salvation in no one else;
for there is no other name under heaven that has been given
among men by which we must be saved.*

Acts 4:12 NASB

*Jesus answered and said unto her, Whosoever drinketh of
this water shall thirst again: but whosoever drinketh of
the water that I shall give him shall never thirst;
but the water that I shall give him shall be in him
a well of water springing up into everlasting life.*

John 4:13, 14 KJV

*G*od's love for you is deeper and more profound than you can imagine. God's love for you is so great that He sent His only Son to this earth to die for your sins and to offer you the priceless gift of eternal life. Now, you must decide whether or not to accept God's gift. Will you welcome Christ into your heart, or will you turn from Him?

Your decision to accept Christ is the pivotal decision of your life. It is a decision that is yours and yours alone. It is a decision with profound consequences, both earthly and eternal. Accept God's gift: Accept Christ today.

It's your heart that Jesus longs for: your will to be
made His own with self on the cross forever,
and Jesus alone on the throne.

Ruth Bell Graham

– A Prayer –

Dear Lord, You gave Your Son that I might have
life eternal. Thank You for this priceless gift and for
the joy I feel in my heart. Today, I will choose to live
in such a way that others, especially my children,
might also accept Christ as their Savior and
that they might see my love for You reflected
through my words and my deeds.

Amen

Asking God

And in that day you will ask Me nothing. Most assuredly,
I say to you, whatever you ask the Father in My name He
will give you. Until now you have asked nothing in
My name. Ask, and you will receive,
that your joy may be full.

John 16:23, 24 NKJV

Do not worry about anything, but
pray and ask God for everything you need,
always giving thanks.

Philippians 4:6 NCV

You do not have, because you do not ask God.

James 4:2 NIV

Ask and it will be given to you; seek and you will find;
knock and the door will be opened to you.
For everyone who asks receives; he who seeks finds;
and to him who knocks, the door will be opened.

Matthew 7:7, 8 NIV

*A*re you a mother whose batteries need recharging? Ask God to recharge them, and He will. Are you worried? Take your concerns to Him in prayer. Are you discouraged? Seek the comfort of God's promises. Do you feel trapped in circumstances that are disheartening, or confusing, or both? Ask God where He wants you to go, and then go there. In all things great and small, seek the transforming power of God's grace. He hears your prayers. And He answers.

We honor God by asking for great things when
they are a part of His promise.
We dishonor Him and cheat ourselves when
we ask for molehills where He has promised mountains.
Vance Havner

– *A Prayer* –
Lord, today I will ask You for the things I need.
In every situation, I will come to You in prayer.
You know what I want, Lord, and more importantly,
You know what I need. Yet even though
I know that You know, I still won't be too timid—
or too busy—to ask.
Amen

Attitude

You were taught, with regard to your former way of life,
to put off your old self, which is being corrupted by its
deceitful desires; to be made new in the attitude of
your minds; and to put on the new self,
created to be like God in true righteousness and holiness.

Ephesians 4:22-24 NIV

Set your mind on the things above,
not on the things that are on earth.

Colossians 3:2 NASB

Your attitude should be the same as that of Christ Jesus:
Who, being in very nature God, did not consider equality
with God something to be grasped, but made himself nothing,
taking the very nature of a servant, being made in human
likeness. And being found in appearance as a man,
he humbled himself and became obedient to death—
even death on a cross!

Philippians 2:5-8 NIV

Finally, brothers, whatever is true, whatever is noble,
whatever is right, whatever is pure, whatever is lovely,
whatever is admirable—if anything is excellent or
praiseworthy—think about such things.

Philippians 4:8 NIV

*T*he Christian life is a cause for celebration, but sometimes we don't feel much like celebrating. In fact, when the weight of the world (and the rigors of motherhood) bear down upon our shoulders, celebration may be the last thing on our minds . . . but it shouldn't be. As God's children—and as the mothers of our own children—we have been blessed beyond measure.

This day is a non-renewable resource—once it's gone, it's gone forever. So celebrate the life that God has given you by thinking optimistically about yourself, your family, and your future. Give thanks to the One who has showered you with blessings, and trust in your heart that He wants to give you so much more.

I could go through this day oblivious to the miracles
all around me, or I could tune in and "enjoy."
Gloria Gaither

– *A Prayer* –
Dear Lord, let me live my life and teach my children
with a spirit of optimism and hope. Whatever
circumstances I face, whether good or bad, triumphal
or tragic, let my response reflect a God-honoring,
Christlike attitude of faith and love for You.
Amen

Blessings

Blessings crown the head of the righteous . . . .

Proverbs 10:6 NIV

The LORD bless thee, and keep thee:
The LORD make his face shine upon thee,
and be gracious unto thee.

Numbers 6:24, 25 KJV

I will make you into a great nation and I will bless you;
I will make your name great, and you will be a blessing.
I will bless those who bless you, and whoever curses you
I will curse; and all peoples on earth
will be blessed through you.

Genesis 12:2, 3 NIV

But my God shall supply all your need
according to his riches in glory by Christ Jesus.

Philippians 4:19 KJV

Unfailing love surrounds those who trust the LORD.

Psalm 32:10 NLT

*I*f you sat down and began counting your blessings, how long would it take? A very, very long time! Your blessings include life, family, friends, freedom, talents, and possessions, for starters. But, your greatest blessing—a gift that is yours for the asking—is God's gift of salvation through Christ Jesus.

Today, give thanks for all of your blessings and share them with your family, with your friends, and with the world. God's love for you is eternal, as are His gifts. And it's never too soon—or too late—to offer Him thanks.

When you and I are related to Jesus Christ,
our strength and wisdom and peace and joy and love
and hope may run out, but His life rushes in to keep us
filled to the brim. We are showered with blessings,
not because of anything we have or have not done,
but simply because of Him.

Anne Graham Lotz

– A Prayer –

Lord, let me be a mother who counts her blessings,
and let me be Your faithful servant as I give praise to
the Giver of all things good. You have richly blessed
my life, Lord. Let me, in turn, be a blessing to my family
and my world—and may the glory be Yours forever.

Amen

Children

Teach [My words] to your children, talking about them
when you sit at home and when you walk along the road,
when you lie down and when you get up. Write them on
the doorframes of your houses and on your gates,
so that your days and the days of your children may be many
in the land that the LORD swore to give your forefathers.

Deuteronomy 11:19-21 NIV

Then He took a child, had him stand among them,
and taking him in His arms, He said to them,
"Whoever welcomes one little child such as this in
My name welcomes Me. And whoever welcomes
Me does not welcome Me, but Him who sent Me."

Mark 9:36, 37 HCSB

Train a child in the way he should go,
and when he is old he will not turn from it.

Proverbs 22:6 NIV

My son, hear the instruction of thy father,
and forsake not the law of thy mother . . . .

Proverbs 1:8 KJV

As mothers, we are aware that God has entrusted us with priceless treasures from above: our children. Every child is a glorious gift from the Father. And, with the Father's gift comes profound responsibilities. Thoughtful mothers understand the critical importance of raising their children with love, with family, with discipline, and with God.

Today, let us pray for our children . . . all of them. Let us pray for our own children and for children around the world. Every child is God's child. May we, as concerned parents, behave—and pray—accordingly.

When Jesus put the little child in the midst of
His disciples, He did not tell the little child to become
like His disciples; He told the disciples to
become like the little child.

Ruth Bell Graham

- A Prayer -

Thank You, Lord, for the priceless gift of my children.
Because I am theirs and they are mine, I am blessed
beyond words. Let me always be mindful of the immense
responsibilities of parenthood, and let me raise
my children to know You and to walk with You always.

Amen

Christ's Love

Who will separate us from the love of Christ?
Will tribulation, or distress, or persecution, or famine, or
nakedness, or peril, or sword? But in all these things
we overwhelmingly conquer through Him who loved us.

Romans 8:35, 37 NASB

I am the good shepherd.
The good shepherd lays down his life for the sheep.

John 10:11 NIV

As the Father hath loved me,
so have I loved you; continue ye in my love.

John 15:9 KJV

And I am convinced that nothing can ever separate us
from his love. Whether we are high above the sky or
in the deepest ocean, nothing in all creation will ever
be able to separate us from the love of God
that is revealed in Christ Jesus our Lord.

Romans 8:38, 39 NLT

This is my commandment, That ye love one another,
as I have loved you. Greater love hath no man than this,
that a man lay down his life for his friends.

John 15:12, 13 KJV

How much does Christ love us? More than we, as mere mortals, can comprehend. His love is perfect and steadfast. Even though we are fallible and wayward, the Good Shepherd cares for us still. Even though we have fallen far short of the Father's commandments, Christ loves us with a power and depth that is beyond our understanding. The sacrifice that Jesus made upon the cross was made for each of us, and His love endures to the edge of eternity and beyond.

Jesus is all compassion. He never betrays us.

Catherine Marshall

– A Prayer –

Dear Lord, I offer thanksgiving and praise for the gift of Your only begotten Son. His love is boundless, infinite, and eternal. And, as an expression of my love for Him, let me share His message with my family, with my friends, and with the world.

Amen

Contentment

Serving God does make us very rich, if we are satisfied
with what we have. We brought nothing into the world,
so we can take nothing out. But, if we have
food and clothes, we will be satisfied with that.

1 Timothy 6:6-8 NCV

Keep your lives free from the love of money,
and be satisfied with what you have. God has said,
"I will never leave you; I will never forget you."

Hebrews 13:5 NCV

I know what it is to be in need, and I know what it is to have
plenty. I have learned the secret of being content in any
and every situation, whether well fed or hungry,
whether living in plenty or in want. I can do
everything through him who gives me strength.

Philippians 4:12, 13 NIV

The LORD will give strength to His people;
The LORD will bless His people with peace.

Psalm 29:11 NKJV

Peace I leave with you, my peace I give unto you;
not as the world giveth, give I unto you.
Let not your heart be troubled, neither let it be afraid.

John 14:27 KJV

The preoccupation with happiness and content-ment is an ever-present theme in the modern world. We are bombarded with messages that tell us where to find peace and pleasure in a world that worships materialism and wealth. But, lasting contentment is not found in material possessions; genuine contentment is a spiritual gift from God to those who trust in Him and follow His commandments. When God dwells at the center of our lives, peace and contentment will belong to us just as surely as we belong to God.

The most powerful life is the most simple life. The most powerful life is the life that knows where it's going, that knows where the source of strength is; it is the life that stays free of clutter and happenstance and hurriedness.

Max Lucado

– A Prayer –

Dear Lord, let me strive to do Your will here on earth, and as I do, let me find contentment and balance. Let me live in the light of Your will and Your priorities for my life. And let me teach my children the peace and contentment that can be theirs through the gift of Your Son.

Amen

Courage

Be of good courage, And He shall strengthen your heart,
All you who hope in the Lord.

Psalm 31:24 NKJV

But Jesus immediately said to them:
"Take courage! It is I. Don't be afraid."

Matthew 14:27 NIV

The Lord himself goes before you and will be with you;
he will never leave you nor forsake you.
Do not be afraid; do not be discouraged.

Deuteronomy 31:8 NIV

He replied, "You of little faith, why are you so afraid?"
Then he got up and rebuked the winds and the waves,
and it was completely calm.

Matthew 8:26 NIV

Fear of man will prove to be a snare,
but whoever trusts in the Lord is kept safe.

Proverbs 29:25 NIV

*T*his world can be a dangerous and daunting place, but Christians have every reason to live courageously. After all, the ultimate battle has already been fought and won on the cross at Calvary. But even the most dedicated Christian mom may find her courage tested by the inevitable disappointments and fears that visit the lives of believers and non-believers alike.

The next time you find your courage tested to the limit, remember to take your fears to God. If you call upon Him, you will be comforted. Whatever your challenge, whatever your trouble, God can handle it. And will.

God did away with all my fear.

Rosa Parks

– A Prayer –

Dear Lord, sometimes this world is a fearful place.
I fear for my family and especially for my children.
Yet, You have promised that You are with us always.
With You as our protector, I am not afraid. Today,
Dear Lord, let me live courageously
as I place my trust in You.

Amen

Discipline

But I discipline my body and bring it into subjection,
lest, when I have preached to others,
I myself should become disqualified.

1 Corinthians 9:27 NKJV

My son, do not despise the Lord's discipline
and do not resent his rebuke, because the Lord disciplines
those he loves, as a father the son he delights in.

Proverbs 3:11, 12 NIV

Discipline your son, for in that there is hope . . . .

Proverbs 19:18 NIV

The fear of the Lord is the beginning of knowledge,
but fools despise wisdom and discipline.

Proverbs 1:7 NIV

Children, obey your parents in all things:
for this is well-pleasing unto the Lord.

Colossians 3:20 KJV

*W*ise mothers teach their children the importance of discipline using both words and examples, but not necessarily in that order.

In Proverbs 28:19, God's message is clear: "He who works his land will have abundant food, but the one who chases fantasies will have his fill of poverty" (NIV). When we work diligently and consistently, we can expect a bountiful harvest. But we must never expect the harvest to precede the labor. Thoughtful parents understand that God doesn't reward laziness or misbehavior. To the contrary, God expects His children (of all ages) to lead disciplined lives that are above reproach.

As we seek to become disciples of Jesus Christ,
we should never forget that the word disciple is directly
related to the word discipline. To be a disciple of
the Lord Jesus Christ is to know his discipline.

Dennis Swanberg

– *A Prayer* –

Dear Lord, give me the wisdom and the strength to be
a disciplined mother. Let me use my time wisely,
and let me teach my children by the faithfulness of
my conduct, today and every day.

Amen

Encouragement

Let's see how inventive we can be in encouraging love
and helping out, not avoiding worshiping together
as some do but spurring each other on.

Hebrews 10:24, 25 MSG

Let the word of Christ dwell in you richly in all wisdom;
teaching and admonishing one another in psalms
and hymns and spiritual songs,
singing with grace in your hearts to the Lord.

Colossians 3:16 KJV

Watch the way you talk. Let nothing foul or
dirty come out of your mouth.
Say only what helps, each word a gift.

Ephesians 4:29 MSG

Reckless words pierce like a sword,
but the tongue of the wise brings healing.

Proverbs 12:18 NIV

Feed the flock of God which is among you . . . .

1 Peter 5:2 KJV

hy did God put you here? One reason is to serve and encourage others, starting with the people who live under your roof. Every member of your family needs a regular supply of encouraging words and pats on the back. And you need the rewards that God gives to enthusiastic moms who are a continual source of encouragement to their loved ones.

Today, look for the good in others—especially your family members—and then, celebrate the good that you find. When you do, you'll be a powerful force of encouragement in your corner of the world . . . and a worthy servant to your God.

So often we think that to be encouragers we have
to produce great words of wisdom when, in fact,
a few simple syllables of sympathy and an arm around
the shoulder can often provide much needed comfort.

Florence Littauer

– A Prayer –

Dear Lord, let me be a source of encouragement to
my family. Just as You have lifted me up,
let me also lift up my loved ones so that they may use
their gifts for the glory of Your Kingdom.

Amen

Enthusiasm

Do your work with enthusiasm.
Work as if you were serving the Lord,
not as if you were serving only men and women.

Ephesians 6:7 NCV

Those who hope in the LORD will renew their strength.
They will soar on wings like eagles; they will run
and not grow weary, they will walk and not be faint.

Isaiah 40:31 NIV

What a help you are to the weak!
How you have saved the arm without strength!

Job 26:2 NASB

For the eyes of the Lord range throughout the earth to
strengthen those whose hearts are fully committed to him.

2 Chronicles 16:9 NIV

Cast thy burden upon the Lord, and he shall sustain thee;
he shall never suffer the righteous to be moved.

Psalm 55:22 KJV

o you see each day as a glorious opportunity to serve God and to do His will? Are you enthused about life, or do you struggle through each day giving scarcely a thought to God's blessings?

If you're a mother with too many demands and too few hours in which to meet them, you are not alone. Motherhood is perhaps the world's most demanding profession. But don't fret. Instead, focus upon God and upon His love for you. Then, ask Him for the strength you need to fulfill your responsibilities. God will give you the energy to do the most important things on today's to-do list . . . if you ask Him. So ask Him.

God is good, and heaven is forever.
And if those two facts don't cheer you up, nothing will.

Marie T. Freeman

– A Prayer –

Lord, let me find my strength in You.
When I feel overwhelmed, let me look to You for
my priorities. Let Your power be my power, Lord,
and let Your way be my way, today and forever.

Amen

Eternal Life

Behold, I tell you a mystery; we will not all sleep,
but we will all be changed, in a moment, in the twinkling of
an eye, at the last trumpet; for the trumpet will sound,
and the dead will be raised imperishable, and we will be
changed. For this perishable must put on the imperishable,
and this mortal must put on immortality. But when this
perishable will have put on the imperishable, and this mortal
will have put on immortality, then will come about
the saying that is written, "DEATH IS SWALLOWED UP
IN VICTORY. "O DEATH, WHERE IS YOUR VICTORY? O DEATH,
WHERE IS YOUR STING?" The sting of death is sin,
and the power of sin is the law; but thanks be to God,
who gives us the victory through our Lord Jesus Christ.

1 Corinthians 15:51–57 NASB

And this is the testimony: that God has given us eternal life,
and this life is in His Son. He who has the Son has life.

1 John 5:11, 12 NKJV

I assure you, anyone who believes in me
already has eternal life.

John 6:47 NLT

*G*od's grace is the ultimate gift, and we owe to Him the ultimate in thanksgiving. Let us praise the Creator for His priceless gift, and let us share the Good News with all who cross our paths.

Christ sacrificed His life on the cross so that we might have eternal life. This gift, freely given from God's only begotten Son, is the priceless possession of everyone who accepts Him as Lord and savior. Claim Christ's gift today.

It is in giving that we receive,
it is in pardoning that we are pardoned,
it is in dying that we are born to eternal life.

St. Francis of Assisi

– A Prayer –

Lord, You have given me the priceless gift of eternal life through Your Son Jesus. Keep the hope of heaven fresh in my heart. May my children see my faith and hear the praise on my lips for You.
May they accept Your gift of eternal life too.

Amen

Evil

For the eyes of the Lord are on the righteous,
and His ears are open to their prayers;
but the face of the Lord is against those who do evil.

1 Peter 3:12 NKJV

Therefore submit to God. Resist the devil and he will flee
from you. Draw near to God and He will draw near to you.
Cleanse your hands, you sinners;
and purify your hearts, you double-minded.

James 4:7, 8 NKJV

Even though I walk through the valley of the shadow
of death, I will fear no evil, for you are with me;
your rod and your staff, they comfort me.

Psalm 23:4 NIV

A fool finds pleasure in evil conduct,
but a man of understanding delights in wisdom.

Proverbs 10:23 NIV

Create in me a clean heart, O God;
and renew a right spirit within me.

Psalm 51:10 KJV

*T*his world is God's creation, and it contains the wonderful fruits of His handiwork. But, it also contains countless opportunities to stray from God's will. Temptations are everywhere, and the devil, it seems, never takes a day off. Our task, as caring mothers, is to do all that we can to protect our families from the evils of the world.

We must recognize evil and fight it. When we observe life objectively, and when we do so with eyes and hearts that are attuned to God's Holy Word, we can no longer be neutral believers. And when we are no longer neutral, God rejoices while the devil despairs.

We are in a continual battle with the spiritual forces
of evil, but we will triumph when we
yield to God's leading and call on
His powerful presence in prayer.

Shirley Dobson

– A Prayer –

Lord, strengthen my walk with You. Evil comes in
many disguises, and sometimes it is only with Your help
that I can recognize right from wrong. Your presence
in my life enables me to choose truth and to live a life
pleasing to You. May I always live in Your presence.

Amen

Failure

Don't pick on people, jump on their failures,
criticize their faults—unless, of course, you want
the same treatment. Don't condemn those who are down;
that hardness can boomerang. Be easy on people;
you'll find life a lot easier.

Luke 6:37 MSG

Have mercy on me, O God, according to your unfailing
love; according to your great compassion blot out
my transgressions. Wash away all my iniquity
and cleanse me from my sin.

Psalm 51:1, 2 NIV

If we confess our sins, he is faithful and just and
will forgive us our sins and purify us
from all unrighteousness.

1 John 1:9 NIV

He who conceals his sins does not prosper,
but whoever confesses and renounces them finds mercy.

Proverbs 28:13 NIV

The occasional disappointments and failures of life are inevitable. Such setbacks are simply the price that we must occasionally pay for our willingness to take risks as we follow our dreams. But even when we encounter bitter disappointments, we must never lose faith.

As parents, we are far from perfect. And, without question, our children are imperfect as well. When we make mistakes, we must correct them and learn from them. And, when our children make mistakes, we must help them do likewise.

How beautiful it is to learn that grace isn't fragile, and that in the family of God we can fail and not be a failure.

Gloria Gaither

– A Prayer –

Dear Lord, sometimes I make mistakes. When I do, help me learn something, help me forgive myself, and help me become a smarter person today than I was yesterday.

Amen

Faith

So then faith comes by hearing,
and hearing by the word of God.

Romans 10:17 NKJV

The Good News shows how God makes people right
with himself—that it begins and ends with faith.
As the Scripture says, "But those who are right
with God will live by trusting in him."

Romans 1:17 NCV

I tell you the truth, if you have faith as small as
a mustard seed, you can say to this mountain,
"Move from here to there" and it will move.
Nothing will be impossible for you.

Matthew 17:20 NIV

Jesus turned and saw the woman and said,
"Be encouraged, dear woman. You are made well
because you believed." And the woman was healed
from that moment on.

Matthew 9:22 NCV

The righteous will live by his faith.

Habakkuk 2:4 NIV

*A*re you a mother whose faith is evident for all to see? Or are you a spiritually shrinking violet? God needs more women who are willing to stand up and be counted for Him.

Every life—including yours—is a series of successes and failures, celebrations and disappointments, joys and sorrows. Every step of the way, through every triumph and tragedy, God will stand by your side and strengthen you . . . if you have faith in Him. Jesus taught His disciples that if they had faith, they could move mountains. You can too, and so can your family . . . if you have faith.

Faith is strengthened only when we ourselves exercise it.

Catherine Marshall

– A Prayer –

Lord, help me to be a mother whose faith is evident to
my family and friends. Help me to remember
that You are always near and that You can overcome
any challenge. With Your love and Your power, Lord,
I will live courageously and share my faith with others,
today and every day.

Amen

Family

*You must choose for yourselves today whom
you will serve . . . as for me and my family,
we will serve the Lord.*

Joshua 24:15 NCV

*Their first responsibility is to show godliness at home
and repay their parents by taking care of them.
This is something that pleases God very much.*

1 Timothy 5:4 NLT

*He who brings trouble on his family
will inherit only wind . . . .*

Proverbs 11:29 NIV

*Honor your father and your mother,
that your days may be long in the land which
the LORD your God gives you.*

Exodus 20:12 RSV

*Listen, my son, to your father's instruction
and do not forsake your mother's teaching.*

Proverbs 1:8 NIV

A loving family is a treasure from God. If God has blessed you with a close knit, supportive clan, offer a word of thanks to your Creator. He has given you one of His most precious earthly possessions. Your obligation, in response to God's gift, is to treat your family in ways that are consistent with His commandments.

When you place God squarely in the center of your family's life—when you worship Him, praise Him, trust Him, and love Him—then He will most certainly bless you and yours in ways that you could have scarcely imagined.

Money can build or buy a house.
Add love to that, and you have a home.
Add God to that, and you have a temple.
You have "a little colony of the kingdom of heaven."

Anne Ortlund

– A Prayer –
Dear Lord, You have given me a wonderful gift:
a loving family. Today and every day,
let me show my family that I love them by
the words that I speak and the way that I behave.

Amen

Fear

For God has not given us a spirit of fear and timidity,
but of power, love, and self-discipline.
So you must never be ashamed to tell others about our Lord.

2 Timothy 1:7, 8 NLT

Don't be afraid, because I am your God.
I will make you strong and will help you;
I will support you with my right hand that saves you.

Isaiah 41:10 NCV

Fear not, for I have redeemed you;
I have called you by your name; You are Mine.

Isaiah 43:1 NKJV

I leave you peace; my peace I give you.
I do not give it to you as the world does.
So don't let your hearts be troubled or afraid.

John 14:27 NCV

. . . Be strong and courageous. Do not be terrified;
do not be discouraged, for the Lord your God
will be with you wherever you go.

Joshua 1:9 NIV

God is willing to protect us. We, in turn, must open ourselves to His protection and His love.

The next time you find your courage tested to the limit, remember to take your fears to God. If you call upon Him, you will be comforted. Whatever your challenge, whatever your trouble, God can handle it. And will.

Worry is a cycle of inefficient thoughts
whirling around a center of fear.

Corrie ten Boom

– A Prayer –
Dear Lord, when I am fearful, keep me mindful that
You are my protector and my salvation.
Thank You, Father, for a perfect love that casts out fear.
Because of You, I can live courageously
and faithfully this day and every day.

Amen

Forgiveness

*Then Peter came to him and asked, "Lord, how often should
I forgive someone who sins against me? Seven times?"
"No!" Jesus replied, "seventy times seven!"*

Matthew 18:21, 22 NLT

*Judge not, and you shall not be judged.
Condemn not, and you shall not be condemned.
Forgive, and you will be forgiven.*

Luke 6:37 NKJV

Hatred stirs up dissention, but love covers over all wrongs.

Proverbs 10:12 NIV

*And when ye stand praying, forgive, if ye have aught
against any; that your Father also which is in heaven may
forgive you your trespasses. But if ye do not forgive,
neither will your Father which is in heaven
forgive your trespasses.*

Mark 11:25, 26 KJV

ven the most mild-mannered moms will, on occasion, have reason to become angry with the inevitable shortcomings of family members and friends. But wise women are quick to forgive others, just as God has forgiven them.

If there exists even one person, alive or dead, whom you have not forgiven (and that includes yourself), follow God's commandment and His will for your life: forgive. Hatred and bitterness and regret are not part of God's plan for your life. Forgiveness is.

Forgiving is a gift God has given us for healing ourselves before we are ready to help anyone else.

Dr. Lewis Smedes

- A Prayer -
Lord, I know that I need to forgive others just as You have forgiven me. Help me to be an example of forgiveness to my children. Keep me mindful, Father, that I am never fully liberated until I have been freed from the chains of bitterness— and that You offer me that freedom through Your Son, Christ Jesus.

Amen

Gifts

God has given gifts to each of you from
his great variety of spiritual gifts. Manage them well
so that God's generosity can flow through you.

1 Peter 4:10 NLT

Now there are varieties of gifts, but the same Spirit.
And there are varieties of ministries, and the same Lord.

1 Corinthians 12:4, 5 NASB

I remind you to fan into flame the gift of God.

2 Timothy 1:6 NIV

Every good and perfect gift is from above,
coming down from the Father of the heavenly lights,
who does not change like shifting shadows.

James 1:17 NIV

His lord said unto him, Well done, thou good and
faithful servant: thou hast been faithful over a few things,
I will make thee ruler over many things:
enter thou into the joy of thy lord.

Matthew 25:21 KJV

*A*ll women possess special gifts and talents; you are no exception. But, your gift is no guarantee of success; it must be cultivated and nurtured; otherwise, it will go unused . . . and God's gift to you will be squandered. Today, accept this challenge: Value the talent that God has given you, nourish it, make it grow, and share it with your family and the world. After all, the best way to say "Thank You" for God's gift is to use it.

The Lord has abundantly blessed me all of my life.
I'm not trying to pay Him back for all of
His wonderful gifts; I just realize
that He gave them to me to give away.

Lisa Whelchel

- A Prayer -
Dear Lord, let me use my gifts, and let me help
my children discover theirs. Your gifts are priceless
and eternal—may we, as your faithful children,
use our own gifts to the glory of Your Kingdom,
today and forever.

Amen

Giving to Others

So when you give to the needy, do not announce it
with trumpets, as the hypocrites do in the synagogues
and on the streets, to be honored by men . . . .
But when you give to the needy, do not let your left hand
know what your right hand is doing, so that your giving
may be in secret. Then your Father,
who sees what is done in secret, will reward you.
Matthew 6:2-4 NIV

The righteous give without sparing.
Proverbs 21:26 NIV

Freely you have received, freely give.
Matthew 10:8 NIV

He that hath two coats, let him impart to him that hath none;
and he that hath meat, let him do likewise.
Luke 3:11 KJV

. . . I tell you the truth, whatever you did for one of
the least of these brothers of mine, you did for me.
Matthew 25:40 NIV

The words of Jesus are clear: "Freely you have received, freely give" (Matthew 10:8 NIV). As followers of Christ, we are commanded to be generous with our friends, with our families, and with those in need. We must give freely of our time, our possessions, and, most especially, our love.

Today, take God's words to heart and make this pledge: Be a cheerful, generous, courageous giver. The world needs your help, and you need the spiritual rewards that will be yours when you give it.

What is your focus today? Joy comes when it is Jesus first, others second . . . then you.

Kay Arthur

- A Prayer -

Lord, You have blessed me with a love that is far beyond my limited understanding. Let me be thankful always, and let me praise You always. Today, let me share those blessings with my family and friends. And let me be a humble giver, Lord, so that all the glory might be Yours.

Amen

God's Commandments

This is how we are sure that we have come to know Him:
by keeping His commands.

1 John 2:3 HCSB

Teach me Your way, O LORD; I will walk in Your truth.

Psalm 86:11 NASB

Blessed are those whose way is blameless,
who walk in the law of the LORD!
Blessed are those who keep his testimonies,
who seek him with their whole heart.

Psalm 119:1, 2 RSV

Trust in the LORD with all your heart and
lean not on your own understanding; in all your ways
acknowledge him, and he will make your paths straight.

Proverbs 3:5, 6 NIV

For this is the love of God,
that we keep his commandments . . . .

1 John 5:3 KJV

God has given us a guidebook for righteous living called the Holy Bible. It contains thorough instructions which, if followed, lead to fulfillment, righteousness and salvation. But, if we choose to ignore God's commandments, the results are as predictable as they are tragic.

As a loving mother, you are keenly aware that God has entrusted you with a profound responsibility: caring for the needs of your family, including their spiritual needs. To fulfill that responsibility, you must study God's Word and live by it. When you do, your example will be a blessing not only to your loved ones, but also to generations yet unborn.

He doesn't need an abundance of words. He doesn't need a dissertation about your life. He just wants your attention. He wants your heart.

Kathy Troccoli

– A Prayer –

Dear Lord, let me obey Your Word, and let me teach my children to do the same. Make me a mother who obeys Your commandments, and let me walk righteously in the footsteps of Your Son, today and every day.

Amen

God's Grace

Let us then approach the throne of grace with confidence,
so that we may receive mercy
and find grace to help us in our time of need.

Hebrews 4:16 NIV

For it is by grace you have been saved, through faith—
and this not from yourselves, it is the gift of God—
not by works, so that no one can boast.

Ephesians 2:8, 9 NIV

But he gives us more grace. That is why Scripture says:
"God opposes the proud but gives grace to the humble."

James 4:6 NIV

You then, my son, be strong in the grace
that is in Christ Jesus.

2 Timothy 2:1 NIV

As God's fellow workers we urge you not to receive
God's grace in vain. For he says, "In the time of my favor
I heard you, and in the day of salvation I helped you.
I tell you, now is the time of God's favor,
now is the day of salvation."

2 Corinthians 6:1, 2 NIV

We have not earned our salvation; it is a gift from God. When we accept Christ as our savior, we are saved by God's grace. Let us praise God for His gift, and let us share the Good News with all who cross our paths. God's grace is the ultimate gift, and we owe to Him the ultimate in thanksgiving. We demonstrate our thanks by sharing His message and His love.

The grace of God is sufficient for all our needs,
for every problem, and for every difficulty,
for every broken heart, and for every human sorrow.

Peter Marshall

– A Prayer –
Dear Lord, Your grace is a gift that cannot be earned.
It is a gift that was given freely when I accepted
Your Son as my personal Savior. Freely have I received
Your gifts, Father. Let me freely share my gifts,
my possessions, my time, my energy, and my faith.
And let my words, my thoughts, my prayers,
and my deeds bring honor to You and to Your Son,
now and forever.

Amen

God's Love

His banner over me was love.

Song of Solomon 2:4 KJV

But God demonstrates his own love for us in this:
While we were still sinners, Christ died for us.

Romans 5:8 NIV

Praise the LORD, all you nations.
For he loves us with unfailing love;
the faithfulness of the LORD endures forever.

Psalm 117:1, 2 NLT

I will sing of the tender mercies of the LORD forever!
Young and old will hear of your faithfulness.
Your unfailing love will last forever.
Your faithfulness is as enduring as the heavens.

Psalm 89:1, 2 NLT

The LORD's lovingkindnesses indeed never cease,
for His compassions never fail.
They are new every morning. Great is Your faithfulness.

Lamentations 3:22, 23 NASB

As a mother, you know the profound love that you hold in your heart for your own children. As a child of God, you can only imagine the infinite love that your Heavenly Father holds for you.

When you embrace God's love, you are forever changed. When you embrace God's love, you feel differently about yourself, your family, your neighbors, and your world. When you embrace God's love, you are compelled to share it with others. When you do so, you are blessed . . . and the Father smiles.

As God's children, we are the recipients of lavish love—
a love that motivates us to keep trusting
even when we have no idea what God is doing.
Beth Moore

- A Prayer -
Thank You, Dear God, for Your love. You are my loving
Father—help me to be a loving mother.
You are my Creator: I will praise You; I will worship You;
and I will love You . . . today, tomorrow, and forever.
Amen

God's Provision

And God will generously provide all you need.
Then you will always have everything you need
and plenty left over to share with others.

2 Corinthians 9:8 NLT

Steep your life in God-reality, God-initiative,
God-provisions. Don't worry about missing out.
You'll find all your everyday human concerns will be met.

Matthew 6:33 MSG

Seek the LORD, and his strength: seek his face evermore.
Remember his marvelous works . . . .

Psalm 105:4, 5 KJV

The LORD is my rock, my fortress and my savior;
my God is my rock in whom I find protection.
He is my shield, the strength of my salvation,
and my stronghold.

Psalm 18:2 NLT

The LORD is my shepherd; I shall not want.

Psalm 23:1 KJV

As a busy woman, you know from firsthand experience that life is not always easy. But as a recipient of God's grace, you also know that you are protected by a loving Heavenly Father. God is always present and always vitally engaged in the events of your life. Reach out to Him, and build your future on the rock that cannot be shaken . . . trust in God and rely upon His provisions. He can provide everything you really need . . . and far, far more.

When God supplies, there is never any depletion of
His resources because His riches are without limit.

Franklin Graham

- A Prayer -
Heavenly Father, You never leave or forsake me.
You are always with me, protecting me
and encouraging me. Whatever this day may bring,
I thank You for Your love and Your strength.
Let me lean upon You, Father,
this day and forever.

Amen

God's Timing

This is what the LORD says:
"In the time of my favor I will answer you,
and in the day of salvation I will help you . . . ."

Isaiah 49:8 NIV

Wait for the LORD;
be strong and take heart and wait for the LORD.

Psalm 27:14 NIV

The steps of the godly are directed by the LORD.
He delights in every detail of their lives.
Though they stumble, they will not fall,
for the LORD holds them by the hand.

Psalm 37:23, 24 NLT

I waited patiently for the LORD;
And He inclined to me, And heard my cry.

Psalm 40:1 NKJV

He has made everything beautiful in its time.
He has also set eternity in the hearts of men;
yet they cannot fathom what God has done
from beginning to end.

Ecclesiastes 3:11 NIV

*I*f you sincerely seek to be a woman of faith, then you must trust God's timing. You will be sorely tempted, however, to do otherwise. Because you are a fallible human being, you are impatient for things to happen. But, God knows better.

God's plan does not always happen in the way that we would like or at the time of our own choosing. Our task—as believing Christians who trust in a benevolent, all-knowing Father—is to wait patiently for God to reveal Himself. And reveal Himself He will. Always. But until God's perfect plan is made known, we must walk in faith and never lose hope. And we must continue to trust Him. Always.

When there is perplexity there is always guidance— not always at the moment we ask, but in good time, which is God's time. There is no need to fret and stew.

Elisabeth Elliot

– A Prayer –

Dear Lord, Your wisdom is infinite, and the timing of Your Heavenly plan is perfect. You have a plan for my life that is grander than I can imagine. When I am impatient, remind me that You are never early or late. You are always on time, Father, so let me trust in You.

Amen

God's Will

The world and its desires pass away,
but the man who does the will of God lives forever.

1 John 2:17 NIV

But what happens when we live God's way?
He brings gifts into our lives, much the same way that
fruit appears in an orchard, things like affection for others,
exuberance about life, serenity. We develop a willingness to
stick with things, a sense of compassion in the heart,
and a conviction that a basic holiness permeates things
and people. We find ourselves involved in loyal
commitments, not needing to force our way in life,
able to marshal and direct our energies wisely.

Galatians 5:22, 23 MSG

Morning by morning he wakens me and
opens my understanding to his will.
The Sovereign LORD has spoke to me, and I have listened.

Isaiah 50:4, 5 NLT

And yet, LORD, you are our Father.
We are the clay, and you are the potter.
We are all formed by your hand.

Isaiah 64:8 NLT

As human beings with limited understanding, we can never fully comprehend the will of God. But as believers in a benevolent God, we must always trust the will of our Heavenly Father.

As this day unfolds, seek God's will for your own life and obey His Word. When you entrust your life to Him completely and without reservation, He will give you the strength to meet any challenge, the courage to face any trial, and the wisdom to live in His righteousness and in His peace.

How often it occurs to me, as it must to you,
that it is far easier simply to cooperate with God!

Beth Moore

– A Prayer –
Lord, let Your will be my will. When I am confused,
give me maturity and wisdom. When I am worried,
give me courage and strength. Let me be
Your faithful servant, Father, always seeking
Your guidance and Your will for my life.

Amen

Golden Rule

See that no one renders evil for evil to anyone,
but always pursue what is good
both for yourselves and for all.

1 Thessalonians 5:15 NKJV

As we have therefore opportunity,
let us do good unto all men,
especially unto them who are of the household of faith.

Galatians 6:10 KJV

May God, who gives this patience and encouragement,
help you live in complete harmony with each other—
each with the attitude of Christ Jesus toward the other.

Romans 15:5 NLT

Be ye therefore merciful, as your Father also is merciful.

Luke 6:36 KJV

Therefore, whatever you want men to do to you,
do also to them, for this is the Law and the Prophets.

Matthew 7:12 NKJV

The words of Matthew 7:12 remind us that, as believers in Christ, we are commanded to treat others as we wish to be treated. This commandment is, indeed, the Golden Rule for Christians of every generation. When we weave the thread of kindness into the very fabric of our lives, we give glory to the One who gave His life for ours.

When we observe God's Golden Rule, we help build His Kingdom here on earth. And, when we share the love of Christ, we share a priceless gift; may we share it today and every day that we live.

The Golden Rule starts at home,
but it should never stop there.

Marie T. Freeman

– *A Prayer* –

Dear Lord, because I expect to be treated with kindness,
let me be kind. Because I wish to be loved,
let me be a loving mother. Because I need forgiveness,
let me be merciful. In all things, Lord, let me live by
the Golden Rule, and let me express my gratitude
to those who offer kindness and generosity to me.

Amen

Gratitude

Everything created by God is good,
and nothing is to be rejected if it is received with gratitude;
for it is sanctified by means of the word of God and prayer.
1 Timothy 4:4, 5 NASB

As you therefore have received Christ Jesus the Lord,
so walk in Him, having been firmly rooted and now being
built up in Him and established in your faith,
just as you were instructed, and overflowing with gratitude.
Colossians 2:6, 7 NASB

Therefore, since we receive a kingdom which cannot be
shaken, let us show gratitude, by which we may offer
to God an acceptable service with reverence and awe . . . .
Hebrews 12:28 NASB

Enter his gates with thanksgiving,
go into his courts with praise.
Give thanks to him and bless his name.
Psalm 100:4 NLT

It is a good thing to give thanks unto the LORD,
and to sing praises unto thy name, O Most High . . . .
Psalm 92:1 KJV

For most of us, life is busy and complicated. As mothers, we have countless responsibilities and obligations. Amid the rush and crush of the daily grind, it is easy to lose sight of God and His blessings. But, when we forget to slow down and say "Thank You" to our Maker, we rob ourselves of His presence, His peace, and His joy.

Instead of ignoring God, we must praise Him many times each day. Then, with gratitude in our hearts, we can face the day's duties with the perspective and power that only He can provide.

Gratitude changes the pangs of memory
into a tranquil joy.

Dietrich Bonhoeffer

- A Prayer -

Lord, You have given me much; when I think of
Your grace and goodness, I am humbled and thankful.
Today, let me praise You not just through my words
but also through my deeds . . . today and every day.

Amen

Happiness

Rejoice always! Pray constantly.
Give thanks in everything,
for this is God's will for you in Christ Jesus.
1 Thessalonians 5:16-18 HCSB

Those who are pure in their thinking are happy,
because they will be with God.
Matthew 5:8 NCV

I've learned by now to be quite content whatever
my circumstances. I'm just as happy with little as with much,
with much as with little. I've found the recipe for being
happy whether full or hungry, hands full or hands empty.
Philippians 4:11, 12 MSG

This is the day the LORD has made;
let us rejoice and be glad in it.
Psalm 118:24 NIV

The LORD is king! Let the earth rejoice!
Psalm 97:1 NLT

Okay, Mom, it's been a typical day. You've cared for your family, worked your fingers to the bone, rushed from Point A to Point Z, and taken barely a moment for yourself. But have you taken time to smile? If so, you're a very wise woman. If not, it's time to slow down, to take a deep breath, and to recount your blessings!

Today, put a smile on your face that stretches all the way down to your heart. When you do, you'll discover that when you smile at God, He smiles back.

God has charged Himself with full responsibility
for our eternal happiness and stands ready
to take over the management of our lives
the moment we turn in faith to Him.

A. W. Tozer

– A Prayer –
Lord, let me be a mother who celebrates life.
Let me rejoice in the gift of this day, and let me
praise You for the gift of Your Son. Let me be
a joyful Christian, Lord, as I share Your Good News
with friends, with family, and with the world.

Amen

Holiness

Rest your hope fully upon the grace that is to be brought to
you at the revelation of Jesus Christ; as obedient children,
not conforming yourselves to the former lusts,
as in your ignorance; but as He who called you is holy,
you also be holy in all your conduct.

1 Peter 1:13-15 NKJV

You will teach me how to live a holy life.
Being with you will fill me with joy;
at your right hand I will find pleasure forever.

Psalm 16:11 NCV

No discipline seems pleasant at the time, but painful.
Later on, however, it produces a harvest of righteousness
and peace for those who have been trained by it.

Hebrews 12:11 NIV

Thus you will walk in the ways of good men and keep
the paths of the righteous. For the upright will live in
the land, and the blameless will remain in it;
but the wicked will be cut off from the land,
and the unfaithful will be torn from it.

Proverbs 2:20-22 NIV

God has given us a guidebook for holy living called the Holy Bible. It is unlike any other book. The Bible contains thorough instructions which, if followed, lead to fulfillment, righteousness and salvation.

As Christians, we are called to study God's Word and to live by it. As parents, we must encourage our children to do the same.

Our souls were made to live in an upper atmosphere,
and we stifle and choke if we live on any lower level.
Our eyes were made to look off from these
heavenly heights, and our vision is distorted
by any lower gazing.

Hannah Whitall Smith

– *A Prayer* –
Lead me, Lord, along Your path, and guide me far
from the temptations of this world.
Let Your Holy Word guide my actions,
and let Your love reside in my heart,
this day and every day.

Amen

Hope

Let us hold on to the confession of our hope
without wavering, for He who promised is faithful.

Hebrews 10:23 HCSB

Happy is he . . . whose hope is in the LORD his God.

Psalm 146:5 KJV

Now faith is the substance of things hoped for,
the evidence of things not seen.

Hebrews 11:1 KJV

I will lift up mine eyes unto the hills,
from whence cometh my help.
My help cometh from the LORD,
which made heaven and earth.

Psalm 121:1, 2 KJV

For we are saved by hope . . . .

Romans 8:24 KJV

*A*re you a hope-filled mom? You should be. After all, God is good; His love endures; and He has offered you the priceless gift of eternal life. And, of course, God has blessed you with a loving family. But sometimes, in life's darker moments, you may lose sight of those blessings, and when you do, it's easy to lose hope.

This world can be a place of trials and tribulations, but as believers, we are secure. Our hope is in God; He has promised us peace, joy, and eternal life. And, of course, God keeps His promises today, tomorrow, and forever, amen!

Oh, remember this: There is never a time when we may not hope in God. Whatever our necessities, however great our difficulties, and though to all appearance help is impossible, yet our business is to hope in God, and it will be found that it is not in vain.

George Mueller

– A Prayer –

Dear Lord, make me a woman who places her hopes in You. If I become discouraged, let me turn to You. If I grow weak, let me seek strength in You. Today and every day, I will trust You, Father, so that my heart will be filled with faith, and with hope, and with love for You.

Amen

Integrity

Till I die, I will not deny my integrity.
I will maintain my righteousness and never let go of it;
my conscience will not reproach me as long as I live.

Job 27:5, 6 NIV

The integrity of the upright shall guide them . . . .

Proverbs 11:3 KJV

A wife of noble character who can find?
She is worth far more than rubies.

Proverbs 31:10 NIV

In everything set them an example by doing what is good.
In your teaching show integrity, seriousness
and soundness of speech that cannot be condemned,
so that those who oppose you may be
ashamed because they have
nothing bad to say about us.

Titus 2:7, 8 NIV

*W*ise mothers teach the importance of integrity. In the Book of Proverbs, we read, "Lying lips are an abomination to the Lord, but those who deal truthfully are His delight" (12:22 NKJV). Clearly, we must strive to be women whose words are pleasing to our Creator. Truth is God's way, and it must be our way, too, even when telling the truth is difficult. As loving mothers, we can do no less.

God never called us to naïveté.
He called us to integrity . . . .
The biblical concept of integrity emphasizes
mature innocence not childlike ignorance.

Beth Moore

- A Prayer -
Dear Lord, Sometimes speaking the truth is difficult,
but when I am weak or fearful, give me the strength
to speak words that are worthy of the One who
created me, so that others might see
Your eternal truth reflected in my words
and my deeds.
Amen

Jesus

Jesus Christ is the same yesterday,
today, and forever.

Hebrews 13:8 HCSB

Jesus said to them, "I am the bread of life;
he who comes to Me will not hunger,
and he who believes in Me will never thirst."

John 6:35 NASB

Jesus answered, "I am the way and the truth and the life.
No one comes to the Father except through me.
If you really knew me, you would know my Father as well.
From now on, you do know him and have seen him."

John 14:6, 7 NIV

At the name of Jesus every knee should bow,
of those in heaven, and of those on earth,
and of those under the earth,
and that every tongue should confess that
Jesus Christ is Lord, to the glory of God the Father.

Philippians 2:10, 11 NKJV

He was the Son of God, but He wore a crown of thorns. He was the Savior of mankind, yet He was put to death on a roughhewn cross made of wood. He offered His healing touch to an unsaved world, and yet the same hands that had healed the sick and raised the dead were pierced with nails. Jesus Christ, the Son of God, was born into humble circumstances. He walked this earth, not as a ruler of men, but as the Savior of mankind. His crucifixion, a torturous punishment that was intended to end His life and His reign, instead became the pivotal event in the history of all humanity.

Jesus is the bread of life. Accept His grace. Share His love. And follow in His footsteps.

When we are in a situation where Jesus is all we have, we soon discover he is all we really need.

Gigi Graham Tchividjian

– A Prayer –

Dear Lord, thank You for Your Son.
Jesus loves me and He shares so much with me.
Let me share His love with others so that through me, they can understand what it means to follow Him.

Amen

Joy

Let the hearts of those who seek the LORD rejoice.
Look to the LORD and his strength; seek his face always.

1 Chronicles 16:10, 11 NIV

Be cheerful no matter what; pray all the time;
thank God no matter what happens.
This is the way God wants you who belong to
Christ Jesus to live.

1 Thessalonians 5:16-18 MSG

Rejoice in the Lord always. I will say it again: Rejoice!

Philippians 4:4 HCSB

I will thank you, LORD with all my heart;
I will tell of all the marvelous things you have done.
I will be filled with joy because of you.
I will sing praises to your name, O Most High.

Psalm 9:1, 2 NLT

. . . these things I speak in the world,
that they might have my joy fulfilled in themselves.

John 17:13 KJV

*A*re you a mom whose joy is evident for all to see? If so, congratulations: You're doing God's will. But if you find yourself feeling discouraged or worse, it's time to slow down and have a quiet conversation with your Creator.

If your heart is heavy, open the door of your soul to the Father and to His only begotten Son. Christ offers you His peace and His joy. Accept it and share it freely, just as Christ has freely shared His joy with you.

Joy is not gush; joy is not mere jolliness.
Joy is perfect acquiescence, acceptance,
and rest in God's will, whatever comes.

Amy Carmichael

– A Prayer –

Dear Lord, You have blessed me with a loving family;
make me thankful, loving, responsible, and wise.
I praise You, Father, for the gift of Your Son and
for the gift of salvation. Let me be a joyful Christian
and a worthy example, this day
and every day that I live.

Amen

Judging Others

Anyone who speaks against his brother or judges him
speaks against the law and judges it.
When you judge the law, you are not keeping it, but sitting in
judgment on it. There is only one Lawgiver and Judge,
the one who is able to save and destroy.
But you—who are you to judge your neighbor?

James 4:11, 12 NIV

Judge not, and you shall not be judged.
Condemn not, and you shall not be condemned.
Forgive, and you will be forgiven.

Luke 6:37 NKJV

Therefore no one is to act as your judge in regard
to food or drink or in respect to a festival
or a new moon or a Sabbath day . . . .

Colossians 2:16 NASB

Therefore judge nothing before the time, until the Lord come,
who both will bring to light the hidden things of darkness,
and will make manifest the counsels of the hearts:
and then shall every man have praise of God.

1 Corinthians 4:5 KJV

ven the most devoted Christians may fall prey to a powerful yet subtle temptation: the temptation to judge others. But as believers, we are commanded to refrain from such behavior. The warning of Matthew 7:1 is clear: "Judge not, that ye be not judged" (KJV).

Have you developed the bad habit of behaving yourself like an amateur judge and jury, assigning blame and condemnation wherever you go? If so, it's time to grow up and obey God. When it comes to judging everything and everybody, God doesn't need your help . . . and He doesn't want it.

Turn your attention upon yourself and beware of
judging the deeds of others, for in judging others
a man labors vainly, often makes mistakes,
and easily sins; whereas, in judging
and taking stock of himself,
he does something that is always profitable.

Thomas à Kempis

– A Prayer –

Lord, it's so easy to judge other people, but it's also easy to misjudge them. Only You can judge a human heart, Lord, so let me love my friends and family members, and let me help them . . . but never let me judge them.

Amen

Kindness

This is what the LORD Almighty says:
Judge fairly and honestly,
and show mercy and kindness to one another.

Zechariah 7:9 NLT

Verily I say unto you,
Inasmuch as ye have done it unto
one of the least of these my brethren,
ye have done it unto me.

Matthew 25:40 KJV

Be kindly affectioned one to another with brotherly love;
in honour preferring one another;
not slothful in business; fervent in spirit;
serving the Lord; rejoicing in hope;
patient in tribulation; continuing instant in prayer . . . .

Romans 12:10-12 KJV

A new commandment I give unto you,
That ye love one another; as I have loved you . . . .

John 13:34 KJV

*W*here does kindness start? It starts in our hearts and works its way out from there. Jesus taught us that a pure heart is a wonderful blessing. It's up to each of us to fill our hearts with love for God, love for Jesus, and love for all people. When we do, we are blessed.

Kindness is God's way. It should be ours, too. So, today, let's be a little kinder than necessary, and let's teach our children the art of kindness through our words and our deeds. Our children are watching . . . and so is God.

As much as God loves to hear our worship and adoration, surely he delights all the more in seeing our gratitude translated into simple kindnesses that keep the chain of praise unbroken, alive in others' hearts.
Evelyn Christenson

- A Prayer -
Lord, make me a loving, encouraging Christian mother. And, let my love for Christ be reflected through the kindness that I show to those who need the healing touch of the Master's hand.
Amen

Laughter

Shout with joy to the Lord, all the earth;
burst into songs and make music. Make music to the Lord
with harps, with harps and the sound of singing.
Blow the trumpets and the sheep's horns;
shout for joy to the Lord the King.

Psalm 98:4-6 NCV

Clap your hands, all you nations;
shout to God with cries of joy.

Psalm 47:1 NIV

A cheerful heart is good medicine . . . .

Proverbs 17:22 NIV

There is a time for everything, and a season for every activity
under heaven . . . a time to weep and a time to laugh,
a time to mourn and a time to dance.

Ecclesiastes 3:1, 4 NIV

This is the day which the LORD hath made;
we will rejoice and be glad in it.

Psalm 118:24 KJV

*M*otherhood is no laughing matter; it should be taken very seriously, up to a point. But no mother's responsibilities should be so burdensome that she forgets to laugh. Laughter is medicine for the soul, but sometimes, amid the stresses of the day, we forget to take our medicine. Instead of viewing our world with a mixture of optimism and humor, we allow worries and distractions to rob us of the joy that God intends for our lives.

As you go about your daily activities, approach life with a smile on your lips and hope in your heart. And laugh every chance you get. After all, God created laughter for a reason . . . and Father indeed knows best. So laugh!

Laughter dulls the sharpest pain and flattens out
the greatest stress. To share it is to give a gift of health.
Barbara Johnson

– A Prayer –
Dear Lord, laughter is Your gift.
Today and every day, put a smile on my face,
and let me share that smile with all who cross my path,
starting with my family . . . and let me laugh.
Amen

Learning

Remember what you are taught.
And listen carefully to words of knowledge.

Proverbs 23:12 ICB

Trust in the LORD with all thine heart;
and lean not unto thine own understanding.
In all thy ways acknowledge him,
and he shall direct thy paths.

Proverbs 3:5, 6 KJV

Teach me, O LORD, the way of Your statutes,
and I shall observe it to the end.

Psalm 119:33 NASB

By wisdom a house is built, and through understanding
it is established; through knowledge its rooms
are filled with rare and beautiful treasures.

Proverbs 24:3, 4 NIV

The fear of the Lord is the beginning of knowledge,
but fools despise wisdom and discipline.

Proverbs 1:7 NIV

Our children need both knowledge and wisdom. Knowledge is found in textbooks. Wisdom, on the other hand, is found in God's Holy Word and in the carefully-chosen words of loving parents and thoughtful teachers. When we give our children the gift of knowledge, we do them a wonderful service. But, when we share the gift of wisdom, we offer a timeless treasure that surpasses knowledge and reshapes eternity.

The wise person gives proper appreciation in his life to his past. He learns to sift the sawdust of heritage in order to find the nuggets that make the current moment have any meaning.

Grady Nutt

– A Prayer –

Lord, You are my Teacher. Help me to be a student of Your Word and a servant of Your will. Let me live by the truth You reveal, let me trust in the wisdom of Your commandments, and let me teach others the glory of Your ways.

Amen

Loving God

Whoever does not love does not know God,
because God is love.

1 John 4:8 NIV

And he has given us this command:
Whoever loves God must also love his brother.

1 John 4:21 NIV

Hear, O Israel: The LORD our God, the LORD is one.
Love the LORD your God with all your heart and with all
your soul and with all your strength. These commandments
that I give you today are to be upon your hearts.
Impress them on your children. Talk about them when you
sit at home and when you walk along the road,
when you lie down and when you get up.

Deuteronomy 6:4-7 NIV

For this is the love of God,
that we keep his commandments . . . .

1 John 5:3 KJV

We love him, because he first loved us.

1 John 4:19 KJV

When we worship God with faith and assurance, when we place Him at the absolute center of our lives, we invite His love into our hearts. In turn, we grow to love Him more deeply as we sense His love for us. St. Augustine wrote, "I love you, Lord, not doubtingly, but with absolute certainty. Your Word beat upon my heart until I fell in love with you, and now the universe and everything in it tells me to love you." Let us pray that we, too, will turn our hearts to our Father, knowing with certainty that He loves us and that we love Him.

A man's spiritual health is exactly proportional
to his love for God.

C. S. Lewis

– A Prayer –
Dear Lord, You have blessed me with a love
that is infinite and eternal. Make me Your loving
servant today and throughout eternity. And,
let me show my love for You by sharing Your message
and Your love with my family, with my friends,
and with the world.

Amen

Loving Others

Above all, love each other deeply,
because love covers a multitude of sins.

1 Peter 4:8 NIV

Love does no wrong to anyone,
so love satisfies all of God's requirements.

Romans 13:10 NLT

But now faith, hope, love, abide these three;
but the greatest of these is love.

1 Corinthians 13:13 NASB

Hatred stirs up dissention, but love covers over all wrongs.

Proverbs 10:12 NIV

A new commandment I give unto you,
That ye love one another; as I have loved you . . . .

John 13:34 KJV

ew things in life are as precious or enduring as a mother's love. Indeed, a mother's love is powerful and priceless. And the familiar words of 1st Corinthians 13 remind us that love is God's commandment. Faith is important, of course. So too is hope. But love is more important still.

Christ showed His love for us on the cross, and, as Christians, we are called upon to return Christ's love by sharing it. We are commanded (not advised, not encouraged . . . commanded!) to love one another just as Christ loved us.

Love is an attribute of God.
To love others is evidence of a genuine faith.

Kay Arthur

– A Prayer –
Dear Lord, I will acknowledge Your love;
I will accept Your love; and I will share Your love.
Let the love that I feel in my heart be expressed
through kind words, good deeds and heartfelt prayers.

Amen

Marriage

Charm is deceptive, and beauty is fleeting;
but a woman who fears the LORD is to be praised.
Give her the reward she has earned . . . .

Proverbs 31:30, 31 NIV

Who can find a virtuous woman?
For her price is far above rubies.

Proverbs 31:10 KJV

Nevertheless, let every one of you in particular
so love his wife even as himself;
and the wife see that she reverence her husband.

Ephesians 5:33 KJV

A virtuous woman is a crown to her husband . . . .

Proverbs 12:4 KJV

Let love and faithfulness never leave you . . .
write them on the tablet of your heart.

Proverbs 3:3 NIV

*W*ho's in charge of your marriage? Is it you, or is it a certain Jewish carpenter from Galilee? A healthy Christian marriage is an exercise in love, fidelity, trust, understanding, forgiveness, caring, sharing, and encouragement. It requires empathy, tenderness, patience, and perseverance. It is the union of two adults, both of whom are willing to compromise and, when appropriate, to apologize.

Few things in life are more sad, or, for that matter, more absurd, than the sight of a grumpy Christian couple bickering about everything in sight. Don't ever be like that. God wants you to experience abundant, joyous relationships, but He expects you to do your fair share of the work. Remember: Joy is a choice—so choose it!

There is nothing wrong with a marriage
that sacrifice wouldn't heal.

Elisabeth Elliot

– A Prayer –

Heavenly Father, You created male and female,
and You created marriage so that man and woman might
join in a new and unique relationship. Help me Lord,
to make my marriage a blessed union that honors
my family, my husband, and You.

Amen

Materialism

Do not love the world or the things in the world.
If anyone loves the world,
the love of the Father is not in him.

1 John 2:15 NKJV

No one can serve two masters.
The person will hate one master and love the other,
or will follow one master and refuse to follow the other.
You cannot serve both God and worldly riches.

Matthew 6:24 NCV

Whoever loves money never has money enough;
whoever loves wealth is never satisfied with his income.

Ecclesiastes 5:10 NIV

And he said unto them, Take heed,
and beware of covetousness: for a man's life consisteth
not in the abundance of the things which he possesseth.

Luke 12:15 KJV

For the love of money is the root of all evil . . . .

1 Timothy 6:10 KJV

How important are our material possessions? Not as important as we might think. In the life of committed Christians, material possessions should play a rather small role, but sometimes, we allow the things that we own to take control of our lives. When we do, we suffer.

Do you find yourself wrapped up in the concerns of the material world? If so, it's time for you and your spouse to sit down and have a heart-to-heart talk about "stuff." When you do, you should reorder your priorities by turning away from materialism and back to God. Then, you can begin storing up riches that will endure throughout eternity: the spiritual kind.

We are made spiritually lethargic
by a steady diet of materialism.

Mary Morrison Suggs

– A Prayer –

Lord, my greatest possession is my relationship with
You through Jesus Christ. You have promised that,
when I first seek Your Kingdom and Your righteousness,
You will give me whatever I need. Let me trust You
completely, Lord, for my needs, both material and
spiritual, this day and always.

Amen

Miracles

But as it is written: "Eye has not seen, nor ear heard,
nor have entered into the heart of man the things which
God has prepared for those who love Him."

1 Corinthians 2:9 NKJV

God verified the message by signs and wonders
and various miracles and by giving gifts of
the Holy Spirit whenever he chose to do so.

Hebrews 2:4 NLT

Jesus said to them,
"I have shown you many great miracles from the Father."

John 10:32 NIV

Search for the LORD and for his strength, and keep on
searching. Think of the wonderful works he has done,
the miracles and the judgments he handed down.

Psalm 105: 4, 5 NLT

Is anything too hard for the Lord?

Genesis 18:14 KJV

Do you believe in God's miraculous provision? You should. But perhaps, as you have faced the inevitable struggles of life, you have, without realizing it, placed limitations on God. To do so is a profound mistake. God's power has no limitations. God can work mighty miracles in your own life if you let Him. Let Him.

When God is involved, anything can happen.
Be open and stay that way. God has a beautiful way
of bringing good vibrations out of broken chords.

Charles Swindoll

- A Prayer -
Dear Lord, absolutely nothing is impossible for You.
Let me trust in Your power and in Your miracles.
When I lose hope, give me faith; when others lose hope,
let me tell them of Your glorious works.
Today, Lord, keep me mindful that You are
a God of infinite possibilities and infinite love.

Amen

Missions

And when the Holy Spirit comes on you,
you will be able to be my witnesses in Jerusalem,
all over Judea and Samaria,
even to the ends of the world.

Acts 1:8 MSG

I will also make You a light of the nations so that
My salvation may reach to the end of the earth.

Isaiah 49:6 NASB

You are the light of the world. A city on a hill cannot be
hidden. Neither do people light a lamp and put it under
a bowl. Instead they put it on its stand, and it gives light to
everyone in the house. In the same way, let your light shine
before men, that they may see your good deeds
and praise your Father in heaven.

Matthew 5:14-16 NIV

As you go, preach this message:
"The kingdom of heaven is near."

Matthew 10:7 NIV

Now then we are ambassadors for Christ . . . .

2 Corinthians 5:20 KJV

Are you a bashful Christian, one who is afraid to speak up for your Savior? Do you leave it up to others to share their testimonies while you stand on the sidelines, reluctant to share yours? Hopefully not.

As believers, we are commanded to share the Good News with our families, with our neighbors, and with the world. Jesus invited His disciples to become fishers of men. We, too, must accept the Savior's invitation, and we must do so today. Tomorrow may indeed be too late.

There is nothing anybody else can do that
can stop God from using us.
We can turn everything into a testimony.

Corrie ten Boom

– A Prayer –
Dear Lord, let me share the Good News of
my salvation, and let me tell of Your love and
of Your grace. Make me a faithful ambassador for You,
Father, and make me a witness to
the transforming power of Your Son.
Amen

Obedience

*Those who obey his commands live in him, and he in them.
And this is how we know that he lives in us:
We know it by the Spirit he gave us.*

1 John 3:24 NIV

*Test all things; hold fast what is good.
Abstain from every form of evil.*

1 Thessalonians 5:21, 22 NKJV

*It is the LORD your God you must follow,
and him you must revere. Keep his commands and obey him;
serve him and hold fast to him.*

Deuteronomy 13:4 NIV

*Jesus replied, "If anyone loves me, he will obey my teaching.
My Father will love him, and we will come to him
and make our home with him."*

John 14:23 NIV

*But if anyone obeys his word, God's love is truly made
complete in him. This is how we know we are in him:
Whoever claims to live in him must walk as Jesus did.*

1 John 2:5, 6 NIV

As loving parents, we must teach our children to obey the rules of society and the laws of God. God's laws are contained in a guidebook for righteous living called the Holy Bible. It contains thorough instructions which, if followed, lead to fulfillment, peace, righteousness, and salvation. But, if we choose to ignore God's commandments, the results are as predictable as they are tragic

Phillips Brooks advised, "Be such a person, and live such a life, that if every person were such as you, and every life a life like yours, this earth would be God's Paradise." And that's sound advice because our families and friends are watching . . . and so, for that matter, is God.

Don't worry about what you do not understand.
Worry about what you do understand
in the Bible but do not live by.

Corrie ten Boom

- A Prayer -

Dear Lord, make me a mother who is obedient to
Your Word. Let me live according to
Your commandments. Direct my path far from
the temptations and distractions of this world.
And, let me discover Your will and follow it, Lord,
this day and always.

Amen

Optimism

But we are hoping for something we do not have yet,
and we are waiting for it patiently.

Romans 8:25 NCV

Make me hear joy and gladness.

Psalm 51:8 NKJV

I can do everything through him who gives me strength.

Philippians 4:13 NIV

Be of good courage, and he shall strengthen your heart,
all ye that hope in the LORD.

Psalm 31:24 KJV

Finally, brethren, whatsoever things are true,
whatsoever things are honest, whatsoever things are just,
whatsoever things are pure, whatsoever things are lovely,
whatsoever things are of good report; if there be any virtue,
and if there be any praise, think on these things.

Philippians 4:8 KJV

As Christian parents, we have every reason to be optimistic about life. As John Calvin observed, "There is not one blade of grass, there is no color in this world that is not intended to make us rejoice." But, sometimes, rejoicing is the last thing on our minds. Sometimes, we fall prey to worry, frustration, anxiety, or sheer exhaustion, and our hearts become heavy. What's needed is plenty of rest, a large dose of perspective, and God's healing touch, but not necessarily in that order.

Make the least of all that goes and the most of all
that comes. Don't regret what is past.
Cherish what you have. Look forward to
all that is to come. And most important of all,
rely moment by moment on Jesus Christ.

Gigi Graham Tchividjian

– A Prayer –

Lord, let me be an expectant Christian. Let me expect
the best from You, and let me look for the best in others.
If I become discouraged, Father, turn my thoughts
and my prayers to You. Let me trust You, Lord,
to direct my life. And, let me be Your faithful, hopeful,
optimistic servant every day that I live.

Amen

Parenting

Their first responsibility is to show godliness at home
and repay their parents by taking care of them.
This is something that pleases God very much.

1 Timothy 5:4 NLT

The good people who live honest lives
will be a blessing to their children.

Proverbs 20:7 NCV

. . . do not provoke your children to anger,
but bring them up in the discipline
and instruction of the Lord.

Ephesians 6:4 NASB

Every kingdom divided against itself will be ruined,
and every city or household divided
against itself will not stand.

Matthew 12:25 NIV

But now faith, hope, love, abide these three;
but the greatest of these is love.

1 Corinthians 13:13 NASB

Every child is different, but every child is similar in this respect: He or she is a priceless gift from the Father above. And, with the Father's gift comes immense responsibilities for moms and dads alike.

Parenting is a full-time job with great responsibilities and the potential for even greater rewards. Our challenge, as parents, is to raise our children lovingly, responsibly, and according to God's commandments. When we do, the difficult job of parenting is made easier, and our families are forever blessed.

As children observe an attitude and spirit of humility
in us, our example will pave the way for them
when they must admit to their heavenly Father
their own desperate need for guidance and forgiveness.

Annie Chapman

- A Prayer -

Heavenly Father, help me to be a responsible, loving, godly mother. Let me teach my children to worship You and to study Your Holy Word. When I am uncertain, Lord, give me wisdom. And, in everything that I do and say, let me be a worthy example to my family every day that I live.

Amen

Patience

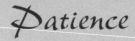

We urge you, brethren, admonish the unruly,
encourage the fainthearted, help the weak,
be patient with everyone.

1 Thessalonians 5:14 NASB

And we desire that each one of you show the same
diligence so as to realize the full assurance of hope
until the end, so that you will not be sluggish,
but imitators of those who through faith
and patience inherit the promises.

Hebrews 6:11, 12 NASB

Patience is better than pride.

Ecclesiastes 7:8 NLT

Better a patient man than a warrior,
a man who controls his temper
than one who takes a city.

Proverbs 16:32 NIV

. . . Those that wait upon the LORD,
they shall inherit the earth.

Psalm 37:9 KJV

The rigors of parenting can test the patience of the most mild-mannered moms. From time to time, even the most mannerly children may do things that worry us, or confuse us, or anger us. Why? Because they are children and because they are human.

As loving parents, we must be patient with our children's shortcomings (just as they, too, must be patient with ours). Sometimes, patience is the price we pay for being responsible mothers, and that's as it should be. After all, think how patient our heavenly Father has been with us.

If only we could be as patient
with other people as God is with us!

Jim Gallery

– A Prayer –

Lord, make me a woman of patience.
When I am hurried, give me peace. When I am
frustrated, give me perspective. When I am angry,
let me turn my heart to You. Today, let me be
a patient Christian, Dear Lord, as I trust in You
and in Your master plan for my life.

Amen

Peace

God has called us to live in peace.

1 Corinthians 7:15 NIV

Live peaceful and quiet lives in all godliness and holiness.

1 Timothy 2:2 NIV

Be perfect, be of good comfort, be of one mind, live in peace;
and the God of love and peace shall be with you.

2 Corinthians 13:11 KJV

Come to me all you who are weary and burdened,
and I will give you rest. Take my yoke upon you
and learn from me, for I am gentle and humble in heart,
and you will find rest for your souls.
For my yoke is easy and my burden is light.

Matthew 11:28-30 NIV

Let the peace of Christ rule in your hearts,
since as members of one body you were called to peace.
And be thankful.

Colossians 3:15 NIV

The beautiful words of John 14:27 give us hope: "Peace I leave with you, my peace I give unto you . . . ." Jesus offers us peace, not as the world gives, but as He alone gives. We, as believers, can accept His peace or ignore it.

Today, as a gift to yourself, to your family, and to your friends, claim the inner peace that is your spiritual birthright: the peace of Jesus Christ. It is offered freely; it has been paid for in full; it is yours for the asking. So ask. And then share.

A great many people are trying to make peace,
but that has already been done. God has not left it for
us to do; all we have to do is to enter into it.

D. L. Moody

– A Prayer –

Dear Lord, let me accept the peace and abundance
that You offer through Your Son Jesus. You are
the Giver of all things good, Father, and You give me
peace when I draw close to You. Help me to trust
Your will, to follow Your commands,
and to accept Your peace, today and forever.

Amen

Persistence

Even though good people may be bothered
by trouble seven times, they are never defeated.

Proverbs 24:16 NCV

Don't look for shortcuts to God.
The market is flooded with surefire, easygoing formulas
for a successful life that can be practiced in your spare time.
Don't fall for that stuff, even though crowds of people do.
The way to life—to God!—
is vigorous and requires total attention.

Matthew 7:13, 14 MSG

For you have need of endurance,
so that when you have done the will of God,
you may receive what was promised.

Hebrews 10:36 NASB

I do not consider myself yet to have taken hold of it.
But one thing I do: Forgetting what is behind and
straining toward what is ahead, I press on toward
the goal to win the prize for which God
has called me heavenward in Christ Jesus.

Philippians 3:13, 14 NIV

As you continue to seek God's purpose for your life, you will undoubtedly experience your fair share of disappointments, detours, false starts, and failures. When you do, don't become discouraged: God's not finished with you yet.

Are you tired? Ask God for strength. Are you discouraged? Believe in His promises. Are you frustrated or fearful? Pray as if everything depended upon God, and work as if everything depended upon you. Then, with God's help, you will find the strength to be the kind of mother who makes her heavenly Father beam with pride.

God never gives up on you,
so don't you ever give up on Him.

Marie T. Freeman

– A Prayer –

Dear Lord, when my responsibilities as a mother seem overwhelming, slow me down and give me perspective. Keep me steady and sure. When I become weary, let me persevere so that, in Your time, I might finish my work here on earth, and that You might then say, "Well done my good and faithful servant."

Amen

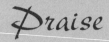

Praise

*Enter into His gates with thanksgiving,
and into His courts with praise. Be thankful to Him,
and bless His name. For the Lord is good;
His mercy is everlasting,
and His truth endures to all generations.*

Psalm 100:4, 5 NKJV

*It is good to give thanks to the Lord,
to sing praises to the Most High.
It is good to proclaim your unfailing love in the morning,
your faithfulness in the evening.*

Psalm 92:1, 2 NLT

*Through Him then, let us continually offer up a sacrifice
of praise to God, that is the fruit of lips that
give thanks to His name.*

Hebrews 13:15 NASB

*In all your ways acknowledge him,
and he will make your paths straight.*

Proverbs 3:6 NIV

God has given you gifts that are beyond measure. He sent His only begotten Son to die for you, and He gave you a family to care for and to love. God has given you another day of life, and He has filled it to the brim with opportunities to celebrate and to serve. What should you do in return for God's priceless gifts? You should praise Him always.

It's our privilege to not only raise our hands in worship but also to combine the visible with the invisible in a rising stream of praise and adoration sent directly to our Father.

Shirley Dobson

- A Prayer -

Heavenly Father, today and every day I will praise You. I come to You with hope in my heart and words of thanksgiving on my lips. Let me follow in Christ's footsteps, and let my thoughts, my prayers, my words, and my deeds praise You now and forever.

Amen

Prayer

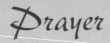

For the eyes of the Lord are over the righteous,
and his ears are open unto their prayers:
but the face of the Lord is against them that do evil.

1 Peter 3:12 KJV

If my people who are called by my name,
will humble themselves and pray and seek my face
and turn from their wicked ways, then will I hear from
heaven and will forgive their sin and will heal their land.

2 Chronicles 7:14 NIV

Ask and it will be given to you; seek and you will find;
knock and it will be opened to you.
For every one who asks receives, and he who seeks finds,
and to him who knocks it will be opened.

Matthew 7:7, 8 NASB

Cast your burden upon the LORD and He will sustain you:
He will never allow the righteous to be shaken.

Psalm 55:22 NASB

When we consult God on an hourly basis, we avail ourselves of His wisdom, His strength, and His love. As Corrie ten Boom observed, "Any concern that is too small to be turned into a prayer is too small to be made into a burden."

Today, instead of turning things over in your mind, turn them over to God in prayer. Instead of worrying about your next decision, ask God to lead the way. Don't limit your prayers to meals or bedtime. Become a woman of constant prayer. God is listening, and He wants to hear from you. Now.

Whatever may be our circumstances in life,
may each one of us really believe that by way
of the Throne we have unlimited power.

Annie Armstrong

– A Prayer –
Dear Lord, I will be a woman of prayer.
I will take everything to You in prayer,
and when I do, I will trust Your answers.
Amen

Renewal

Do you not know? Have you not heard?
The Everlasting God, the LORD, the Creator of
the ends of the earth does not become weary or tired.
His understanding is inscrutable. He gives strength to
the weary, and to him who lacks might He increases power.
Though youths grow weary and tired, and vigorous young
men stumble badly, yet those who wait for the LORD will gain
new strength; they will mount up with wings like eagles,
they will run and not get tired,
they will walk and not become weary.

Isaiah 40:28-31 NASB

When doubts filled my mind,
your comfort gave me renewed hope and cheer.

Psalm 94:19 NLT

I will give you a new heart and put a new spirit in you . . . .

Ezekiel 36:26 NIV

. . . let the hearts of those who seek the LORD rejoice.
Look to the LORD and his strength; seek his face always.

1 Chronicles 16:10, 11 NIV

*E*ven the most inspired Christian women can, from time to time, find themselves running on empty. The demands of daily life can drain us of our strength and rob us of the joy that is rightfully ours in Christ. Are you tired or troubled? Turn your heart toward God in prayer. Are you weak or worried? Take the time—or, more accurately, make the time—to delve deeply into God's Holy Word. Are you spiritually depleted? Call upon fellow believers to support you, and call upon Christ to renew your spirit and your life. When you do, you'll discover that the Creator of the universe stands always ready and always able to create a new sense of wonderment and joy in you.

Whoever you are, whatever your condition or circumstance, whatever your past or problem, Jesus can restore you to wholeness.

Anne Graham Lotz

- A Prayer -

Lord, I am an imperfect mother. Sometimes, I become overwhelmed by the demands of the day. When I feel tired or discouraged, renew my strength. When I am worried, let me turn my thoughts and my prayers to You. Let me trust Your promises, Dear Lord, and let me accept Your unending love, now and forever.

Amen

Sadness

May the God of hope fill you with all joy and peace
as you trust in him, so that you may overflow
with hope by the power of the Holy Spirit.

Romans 15:13 NIV

. . . but we glory in tribulations also;
knowing that tribulation worketh patience;
and patience, experience; and experience, hope . . . .

Romans 5:3, 4 KJV

Blessed are those who mourn, for they will be comforted.

Matthew 5:4 NIV

They that sow in tears shall reap in joy.

Psalm 126:5 KJV

For thou wilt light my candle:
the LORD my God will enlighten my darkness.

Psalm 18:28 KJV

*G*rief is the price that life periodically exacts from those who live long and love deeply. When we lose a loved one, or when we experience any other profound loss, darkness overwhelms us for a while, and it seems as if we cannot summon the strength to face another day—but, with God's help, we can. During times of heartache, we can turn to God, first for solace and then for renewal. When we do, He comforts us and, in time, He heals us.

Our tears do not fall without the hand of God
catching every one.

Kathy Troccoli

– A Prayer –
Dear Heavenly Father, on those days when
I am troubled, You comfort me if I turn my thoughts
and prayers to You. When I am afraid,
You protect me. When I am discouraged,
You lift me up. You are my unending source of strength,
Lord. In every circumstance, let me trust
Your plan and Your will for my life.
Amen

Salvation

Sing to the LORD, all the earth;
proclaim his salvation day after day.

1 Chronicles 16:23 NIV

And we have seen and testify that the Father
has sent his Son to be the Savior of the world.

1 John 4:14 NIV

Everyone who calls on the name of the Lord will be saved.

Romans 10:13 NIV

I tell you the truth, he who believes has everlasting life.

John 6:47 NIV

For it is by grace you have been saved, through faith—
and this not from yourselves, it is the gift of God . . . .

Ephesians 2:8 NIV

How marvelous it is that the Son of God walked among us. Had He not chosen to do so, we might feel removed from a distant Creator. But ours is not a distant God. Ours is a God who understands—far better than we ever could—the essence of what it means to be human. God understands our hopes, our fears, and our temptations. He understands what it means to be angry and what it costs to forgive. He knows the heart, the conscience, and the soul of every person who has ever lived, including you.

God has a plan of salvation that is intended for you. Accept it. Accept God's gift through the person of His Son Christ Jesus, and then rest assured: God walked among us so that you might have eternal life; amazing though it may seem, He did it for you.

The essence of salvation is an about-face from self-centeredness to God-centeredness.

Henry Blackaby

– A Prayer –
Lord, I'm only here on earth for a brief visit. Heaven is my real home. You've given me the gift of eternal life through Your Son Jesus. I accept Your gift, Lord. And I will share Your Good News so that my family and friends, too, might come to know Christ's healing touch.

Amen

Scripture

For the word of God is living and effective and
sharper than any two-edged sword,
penetrating as far as to divide soul, spirit, joints,
and marrow; it is a judge of the ideas and
thoughts of the heart.

Hebrews 4:12 HCSB

For as the rain comes down, and the snow from heaven,
and do not return there, but water the earth,
and make it bring forth and bud, that it may give seed to
the sower and bread to the eater, so shall My word be
that goes forth from My mouth; it shall not return
to Me void, but it shall accomplish what I please,
and it shall prosper in the thing for which I sent it.

Isaiah 55:10, 11 NKJV

Every word of God is flawless;
he is a shield to those who take refuge in him.

Proverbs 30:5 NIV

Shew me thy ways, O LORD; teach me thy paths.
Lead me in thy truth, and teach me:
for thou art the God of my salvation;
on thee do I wait all the day.

Psalm 25:4, 5 KJV

Is God's Word a lamp that guides your path? Is God's Word your indispensable compass for everyday living, or is it relegated to Sunday morning services? Do you read the Bible faithfully or sporadically? The answer to these questions will determine the direction of your thoughts, the direction of your day, and the direction of your life.

God's Word can be a roadmap to a place of righteousness and abundance. Make it your roadmap, today, tomorrow, and every day of your life—and then walk confidently in the footsteps of God's only begotten Son.

Approach the Scriptures not so much as a manual of
Christian principles but as the testimony of
God's friends on what it means to walk with him
through a thousand different episodes.

John Eldredge

– A Prayer –
Heavenly Father, Your Holy Word is a light unto
the world; let me study it, trust it, and share it
with all who cross my path. In all that I do,
help me be a worthy witness for You as I share
the Good News of Your perfect Son
and Your perfect Word.

Amen

Seeking God

My soul thirsts for God, for the living God.

Psalm 42:2 NASB

Speak, Lord. I am your servant and I am listening.

1 Samuel 3:10 NCV

The LORD is with you when you are with him.
If you seek him, he will be found by you . . . . .

2 Chronicles 15:2 NIV

The LORD is good to those whose hope is in him,
to the one who seeks Him . . . .

Lamentations 3:25 NIV

But seek first the kingdom of God and His righteousness,
and all these things shall be added to you.

Matthew 6:33 NKJV

Sometimes, in the crush of our daily duties, God seems far away. But He is not. God is everywhere you have ever been and everywhere you will ever go. He is with you night and day; He knows your every thought; He hears your every heartbeat.

When you earnestly seek God, you will find Him because He is here, waiting patiently for you to reach out to Him . . . right here . . . right now.

We rarely discover anything monumental about
God without discovering something momentous
about ourselves. With every revelation comes
an invitation to adjust our lives to what we have seen.

Beth Moore

– A Prayer –
How comforting it is, Dear Lord, to know that
if I seek You, I will find You. You are with me, Father,
every step that I take. Let me reach out to You,
and let me praise You for revealing Your Word,
Your way, and Your love.

Amen

Serving Others

Sitting down, He called the Twelve and said to them,
"If anyone wants to be first,
he must be last of all and servant of all."

Mark 9:35 HCSB

But he who is greatest among you
shall be your servant.
And whoever exalts himself will be humbled,
and he who humbles himself will be exalted.

Matthew 23:11, 12 NKJV

Suppose a brother or a sister is without clothes and
daily food. If one of you says to him,
"Go, I wish you well; keep warm and well fed,"
but does nothing about his physical needs, what good is it?

James 2:15, 16 NIV

Shepherd God's flock, for whom you are responsible.
Watch over them because you want to,
not because you are forced. That is how God wants it.
Do it because you are happy to serve.

1 Peter 5:2 NCV

*I*f you genuinely seek to discover God's unfolding purpose for your life, you must ask yourself this question: "How does God want me to serve others?"

Every single day of your life, including this one, God will give you opportunities to serve Him by serving His children. Welcome those opportunities with open arms. They are God's gift to you, His way of allowing you to achieve greatness in His kingdom.

Christians are like the flowers in a garden:
they have upon them the dew of heaven, which,
being shaken by the wind, they let fall
at each other's roots, whereby they are jointly nourished.

John Bunyan

– *A Prayer* –

Dear Lord, as a mother, I am an example to every
member of my family. Give me a servant's heart
and make me a faithful steward of my gifts.
Let me follow in the footsteps of Your Son Jesus
who taught us by example that to be great in Your eyes,
Lord, is to serve others humbly, faithfully, and lovingly.

Amen

Sharing

And God will generously provide all you need.
Then you will always have everything you need
and plenty left over to share with others.

2 Corinthians 9:8 NLT

In everything I did, I showed you that by this kind
of hard work we must help the weak,
remembering the words the Lord Jesus himself said:
"It is more blessed to give than to receive."

Acts 20:35 NIV

He that hath two coats,
let him impart to him that hath none;
and he that hath meat, let him do likewise.

Luke 3:11 KJV

The righteous give without sparing.

Proverbs 21:26 NIV

The thread of generosity is woven—completely and inextricably—into the very fabric of Christ's teachings. When we walk each day with Christ—and obey the commandments found in God's Holy Word—we become generous servants to those who need our help.

Just as Christ is the ultimate shepherd to His flock, so should we care for those whom God has seen fit to place along our paths. When we give of ourselves and our possessions—and when we do so cheerfully and humbly—we share a priceless gift: the love of Christ. May we share it today and every day that we live.

We are only fully alive when we're helping others.

Rick Warren

- A Prayer -

Dear Lord, Your Word tells me that it is more blessed to give than to receive. Make me a faithful steward of the gifts You have given me, and let me share those gifts generously with others, today and every day that I live.

Amen

Strength

Be strong and brave, and do the work.
Don't be afraid or discouraged, because the Lord God,
my God, is with you. He will not fail you or leave you."

1 Chronicles 28:20 NCV

And He said to me, "My grace is sufficient for you,
for My strength is made perfect in weakness."

2 Corinthians 12:9 NKJV

. . . I do not consider myself yet to have taken hold of it.
But one thing I do: Forgetting what is behind and straining
toward what is ahead, I press on toward the goal to win
the prize for which God has called me
heavenward in Christ Jesus.

Philippians 3:13, 14 NIV

The LORD is my strength and my song . . . .

Exodus 15:2 NIV

God is our refuge and strength,
a very present help in trouble.

Psalm 46:1 KJV

*W*here do you turn for strength? Do you depend upon the world's promises or, for that matter, upon your own resources? Or do you turn toward God for the wisdom and strength to meet the challenges of the coming day? The answer should be obvious: God should come first.

Today and every day, spend time with your Creator. Offer Him your prayers and study His Word. When you offer God the firstfruits of your day, you gain wisdom, perspective, and strength.

God is great and God is powerful,
but we must invite him to be powerful in our lives.
His strength is always there, but it's up to us to provide
a channel through which that power can flow.

Bill Hybels

– A Prayer –
Dear Lord, being a mother isn't easy.
Sometimes, I am worried; sometimes I am weary;
and sometimes I become discouraged.
When I am worried, give me faith.
When my responsibilities seem overwhelming,
give me strength and perspective.
And keep me mindful, Lord, that You are
the ultimate source of my hope, my strength,
my peace, and my salvation.

Amen

Temper

Patient people have great understanding,
but people with quick tempers show their foolishness.

Proverbs 14:29 NCV

. . . do not let the sun go down on your anger,
and do not give the devil an opportunity.

Ephesians 4:26, 27 NASB

Refrain from anger and turn from wrath;
do not fret—it leads only to evil.

Psalm 37:8 NIV

People with quick tempers cause trouble,
but those who control their tempers stop a quarrel.

Proverbs 15:18 NCV

But now faith, hope, love, abide these three;
but the greatest of these is love.

1 Corinthians 13:13 NASB

*D*o you exercise firm control over your temper? Hopefully so. Temper tantrums are usually unproductive, unattractive, unforgettable, and unnecessary. Perhaps that's why Proverbs 16:32 states, "Controlling your temper is better than capturing a city" (NCV).

If you've allowed anger to become a regular visitor at your house, pray for wisdom, for patience, and for a heart that is so filled with love and forgiveness that it contains no room for bitterness. God will help you terminate your tantrums if you ask Him to. And God can help you perfect your ability to be a patient parent if you ask Him to. So ask Him, and then wait patiently for the ever-more-patient you to arrive.

Why lose your temper if, by doing so, you offend God,
annoy other people, give yourself a bad time . . .
and, in the end, have to find it again?

Josemaria Escriva

- A Prayer -
Lord, sometimes, it is so easy to lose my temper and
my perspective. When anger burdens my soul,
enable me to calm myself and to be a witness to
Your truth and righteousness. Let my children
see me as a model of kindness and forgiveness,
today and every day.

Amen

Thanksgiving

Make a joyful noise unto the LORD all ye lands.
Serve the LORD with gladness: come before his presence
with singing. Know ye that the LORD he is God:
it is he that hath made us, and not we ourselves;
we are his people and the sheep of his pasture.
Enter into his gates with thanksgiving, and into his courts
with praise; be thankful unto him and bless his name.
For the LORD is good; his mercy is everlasting;
and his truth endureth to all generations.

Psalm 100 KJV

Let the peace of Christ rule in your hearts,
since as members of one body you were called to peace.
And be thankful.

Colossians 3:15 NIV

It is good to give thanks to the Lord, to sing praises to
the Most High. It is good to proclaim your unfailing love
in the morning, your faithfulness in the evening.

Psalm 92:1, 2 NLT

Come, let us sing to the LORD! Let us give a joyous shout to
the rock of our salvation! Let us come before him
with thanksgiving. Let us sing him psalms of praise.

Psalm 95:1, 2 NLT

*S*ometimes, life here on earth can be complicated, demanding, and frustrating. When the demands of life leave us rushing from place to place with scarcely a moment to spare, we may fail to pause and thank our Creator for the countless blessings He bestows upon us. But, whenever we neglect to give proper thanks to the Giver of all things good, we suffer because of our misplaced priorities.

Are you taking God's gifts for granted? If so, you are doing a disservice to your Creator and yourself. And the best way to resolve that problem is to make this day a time for celebration and praise. Starting now.

The devil moves in when a Christian starts to complain,
but thanksgiving in the Spirit defeats
the devil and glorifies the Lord.

Warren Wiersbe

- A Prayer -
Lord, let me be a thankful Christian.
Your blessings are priceless and eternal.
I praise You, Lord, for Your gifts and,
most of all, for Your Son.

Amen

Today

Rejoice in the Lord always; again I will say, rejoice!

Philippians 4:4 NASB

While it is daytime, we must continue doing the work
of the One who sent me.
Night is coming, when no one can work.

John 9:4 NCV

Encourage one another daily, as long as it is Today . . . .

Hebrews 3:13 NIV

The Lord reigns; Let the earth rejoice.

Psalm 97:1 NKJV

This is the day the LORD has made.
We will rejoice and be glad in it.

Psalm 118:24 NLT

What do you expect from the day ahead? Are you expecting God to do wonderful things, or are you living beneath a cloud of apprehension and doubt?

For Christian believers, every day begins and ends with God and His Son. Christ came to this earth to give us abundant life and eternal salvation. We give thanks to our Maker when we treasure each day and use it to the fullest. Today, let us give thanks for the gift of life and for the One who created it. And then, let's use this day—a precious gift from the Father above—to serve our Savior and to share His Good News with all who cross our paths.

Submit each day to God,
knowing that He is God over all your tomorrows.

Kay Arthur

- A Prayer -

Dear Lord, You have given me another day of life;
let me celebrate this day, and let me use it according to
Your plan. I come to You today with faith in my heart
and praise on my lips. I praise You, Father, for the gift
of life and for the friends and family members who make
my life rich. Enable me to live each moment to
the fullest, totally involved in Your will.

Amen

Troubles

Let not your heart be troubled:
ye believe in God, believe also in me.

John 14:1 KJV

I have told you these things,
so that in me you may have peace.
In this world you will have trouble.
But take heart! I have overcome the world.

John 16:33 NIV

Even though good people may be bothered
by trouble seven times, they are never defeated.

Proverbs 24:16 NCV

Come to me all you who are weary and burdened,
and I will give you rest. Take my yoke upon you
and learn from me, for I am gentle and humble in heart,
and you will find rest for your souls.
For my yoke is easy and my burden is light.

Matthew 11:28-30 NIV

From time to time, all of us face adversity, hardship, disappointment, and loss. Old Man Trouble pays periodic visits to each of us; none of our families are exempt. When we are troubled, God stands ready and willing to protect us. Our responsibility, of course, is to ask Him for protection.

Psalm 147 promises, "He heals the brokenhearted, and binds their wounds" (v. 3). When we are troubled, we must call upon God, and, in His own time and according to His own plan, He will heal us.

> Looking back, I can see that the most exciting events of my life have all risen out of trouble.
>
> *Catherine Marshall*

– A Prayer –

Heavenly Father, You are my strength and my refuge. As I journey through this day, I know that I may encounter disappointments and losses. When I am troubled, let me turn to You. Keep me steady, Lord, and renew a right spirit inside of me this day and forever.

Amen

Trust in God

He heeded their prayer, because they put their trust in him.
1 Chronicles 5:20 NKJV

And God, in his mighty power, will protect you until
you receive this salvation, because you are trusting him.
1 Peter 1:5 NLT

Do not let your hearts be troubled. Trust in God;
trust also in me. In my Father's house are many rooms;
if it were not so, I would have told you.
I am going there to prepare a place for you.
John 14:1, 2 NIV

The LORD is my rock, and my fortress, and my deliverer; my
God, my strength, in whom I will trust . . . .
Psalm 18:2 KJV

. . . the Lord's unfailing love surrounds
the man who trusts in him.
Psalm 32:10 NIV

here will you place your trust today? Will you trust in the ways of the world, or will you trust in the Word and the will of your Creator? If you aspire to do great things for God's kingdom, you will trust Him completely.

Do you seek God's blessings for yourself and for your family? Then trust Him. Trust God with every aspect of your life. When you do, God will bless you and yours in ways that you never could have imagined.

How changed our lives would be if we could only fly through the days on wings of surrender and trust!
Hannah Whitall Smith

— A Prayer —
Lord, when I trust in the things of this earth,
I will be disappointed. But, when I put my faith in You,
I am secure. In every aspect of my life, Father,
let me place my hope and my trust in
Your infinite wisdom and Your boundless grace.
Amen

Truth

I have no greater joy than this,
to hear of my children walking in the truth.

3 John 1:4 NASB

But when the Spirit of truth comes,
he will lead you into all truth.

John 16:13 NCV

These are the things you are to do:
Speak the truth to each other, and render
true and sound judgment in your courts . . . .

Zechariah 8:16 NIV

Jesus answered, "I am the way and the truth and the life.
No one comes to the Father except through me."

John 14:6 NIV

And ye shall know the truth,
and the truth shall make you free.

John 8:32 KJV

*G*od is vitally concerned with truth. His Word teaches the truth; His Spirit reveals the truth; His Son leads us to the truth. When we open our hearts to God, and when we allow His Son to rule over our thoughts and our lives, God reveals Himself, and we come to understand the truth about ourselves and the Truth about God's gift of grace.

The familiar words of John 8:32 remind us that God's truth does, indeed, make us free. May we, as believers, seek His truth and live by it, this day and forever.

Jesus differs from all other teachers;
they reach the ear, but he instructs the heart;
they deal with the outward letter,
but he imparts an inward taste for the truth.

C. H. Spurgeon

- A Prayer -
Dear Lord, You have shown me the truth and
the way through Your Son Jesus. Let me trust
the promises of the Savior, and let me share
His truth with my family and friends,
today and every day that I live.

Amen

Wisdom

Do not deceive yourselves. If any one of you thinks
he is wise by the standards of this age, he should become
a "fool" so that he may become wise.
For the wisdom of this world is foolishness in God's sight.

1 Corinthians 3:18, 19 NIV

The fear of the LORD is the beginning of wisdom;
a good understanding have all those who do
His commandments. His praise endures forever.

Psalm 111:10 NKJV

Are there those among you who are truly wise and
understanding? Then they should show it by living right and
doing good things with a gentleness that comes from wisdom.

James 3:13 NCV

For the LORD gives wisdom,
and from his mouth come knowledge and understanding.

Proverbs 2:6 NIV

But if any of you lacks wisdom, let him ask of God,
who gives to all generously and without reproach,
and it will be given to him.

James 1:5 NASB

Sometimes, amid the demands of daily life, we lose perspective. Life seems out of balance, and the pressures of everyday living seem overwhelming. What's needed is a fresh perspective, a restored sense of balance . . . and God's wisdom.

If we call upon the Lord and seek to see the world through His eyes, He will give us guidance, wisdom and perspective. When we make God's priorities our priorities, He will lead us according to His plan and according to His commandments. When we study God's Word, we are reminded that God's reality is the ultimate reality. May we live accordingly.

Knowledge can be found in books or in school.
Wisdom, on the other hand, starts with God . . .
and ends there.

Marie T. Freeman

– A Prayer –

Lord, make me a woman of wisdom and discernment.
I seek wisdom, Lord, not as the world gives,
but as You give. Lead me in Your ways and
teach me from Your Word so that, in time,
my wisdom might glorify Your Kingdom and Your Son.

Amen

Work

Work hard so God can approve you.
Be a good worker, one who does not need to be ashamed
and who correctly explains the word of truth

2 Timothy 2:15 NLT

Whatever your hand finds to do,
do it with all your might . . . .

Ecclesiastes 9:10 NIV

Whatever you do, do your work heartily,
as for the Lord rather than for men.

Colossians 3:23 NASB

My heart took delight in all my work . . . .

Ecclesiastes 2:10 NIV

But as for you, be strong and do not give up,
for your work will be rewarded.

2 Chronicles 15:7 NIV

*M*otherhood is not only the most rewarding profession, it is also the most demanding. Mothers seldom, if ever, get a day off. And when the sun goes down, there is no rest for Mom until her head hits the pillow.

And does all this hard work pay off? Of course it does . . . every time the woman of the house hears those glorious words, "I love you Mom!"

As a mother, my job is to take care of the possible
and trust God with the impossible.

Ruth Bell Graham

– A Prayer –

Heavenly Father, You know that motherhood is
difficult work. When I am tired, give me strength.
When I become frustrated, give me patience.
When I lose sight of Your purpose for my life,
give me a passion for my daily responsibilities.
Let me raise my children to be Your loving,
faithful servants, and let all the honor
and glory be Yours.

Amen

Worry

Now it happened as they went that He entered
a certain village; and a certain woman named Martha
welcomed Him into her house. And she had a sister called
Mary, who also sat at Jesus' feet and heard His word.
But Martha was distracted with much serving, and she
approached Him and said, "Lord, do You not care that my
sister has left me to serve alone? Therefore tell her
to help me." And Jesus answered and said to her,
"Martha, Martha, you are worried and troubled about
many things. But one thing is needed, and Mary has chosen
that good part, which will not be taken away from her."

Luke 10:38-42 NKJV

Therefore do not worry about tomorrow,
for tomorrow will worry about itself.
Each day has enough trouble of its own.

Matthew 6:34 NIV

Yea, though I walk through the valley of the shadow of death,
I will fear no evil: for thou art with me;
thy rod and thy staff they comfort me.

Psalm 23:4 KJV

*I*f you are like most mothers, it is simply a fact of life: from time to time, you worry. You worry about your children, about your health, about finances, about safety, about relationships, about family, and about countless other challenges of life, some great and some small.

Where is the best place to take your worries? Take them to God. Take your troubles to Him, and your fears, and your sorrows. Seek protection from the One who cannot be moved.

God is bigger than your problems.
Whatever worries press upon you today,
put them in God's hands and leave them there.

Billy Graham

– A Prayer –

Lord, You understand my worries and my fears,
and You forgive me when I am weak.
When my faith begins to waver, help me to trust
You more. Then, with Your Holy Word on my lips
and with the love of Your Son in my heart,
let me live courageously, faithfully, prayerfully,
and thankfully today and every day.

Amen

Worship

But the hour is coming, and now is, when the true
worshipers will worship the Father in spirit and truth;
for the Father is seeking such to worship Him. God is Spirit,
and those who worship Him must worship in spirit and truth.

John 4:23, 24 NKJV

Worship the Lord your God and . . . serve Him only.

Matthew 4:10 HCSB

Happy are those who hear the joyful call to worship,
for they will walk in the light of your presence, LORD.

Psalm 89:15 NLT

O come, let us sing unto the LORD:
let us make a joyful noise to the rock of our salvation.
Let us come before his presence with thanksgiving,
and make a joyful noise unto him with psalms.

Psalm 95:1, 2 KJV

I was glad when they said unto me,
Let us go into the house of the LORD.

Psalm 122:1 KJV

How can we ensure that we cast our lot with God? We do so, in part, by the practice of regular, purposeful worship with our families. When we worship God faithfully and fervently, we are blessed. When we fail to worship God, for whatever reason, we forfeit the spiritual gifts that He intends for us.

We must worship our heavenly Father, not just with our words, but also with deeds. We must honor Him, praise Him, and obey Him. As we seek to find purpose and meaning for our lives, we must first seek His purpose and His will. For believers, God comes first. Always first.

Spiritual worship is focusing all we are on all He is.

Beth Moore

– A Prayer –

Dear Lord, this world is a place of distractions and temptations. But when I worship You, Father, You set my path—and my heart—straight. Let this day and every day be a time of worship. Help me find quiet moments to praise You for Your blessings, for Your love, and for Your Son.

Amen